Sheila,

We love you very much and are pleased to be with this day.

The Conn's
April 18, 1977

MOMENTS OF DECISION

MOMENTS OF DECISION

profiles of great men and women

by the Daughters of St. Paul

ST. PAUL EDITIONS

NIHIL OBSTAT:
  John G. Hogan

IMPRIMATUR:
✠Humberto Cardinal Medeiros
  Archbishop of Boston

May 8, 1975

Printed in U.S.A. by the Daughters of St. Paul
50 St. Paul's Ave., Boston, Ma. 02130

Printed in U.S.A. by the Daughters of St. Paul
50 St. Paul's Ave., Boston, Ma. 02130

The Daughters of St. Paul are an international religious congregation serving the Church with the communications media.

Contents

woman
of
fire

Catherine Benincasa was born on March 25, the feast of the Annunciation of the Blessed Virgin Mary, in the distant year of 1347. She was the twenty-fourth of the twenty-five children with which God blessed the marriage of Giacomo and Lapa Benincasa. Wedged in as she was among so many, Catherine could easily have become lost in the crowd, a mediocre or average Christian who did only what was required of her. But Catherine was nothing of that sort. Keen intelligence, strong determination and a passionate love of God combined together to make of her what few women of history have been.

From early years she was held fast by a truth that Christ had spoken to her deep within the recesses of her being: "You are that which is not; I am He who is. If you have this knowledge in your soul, you will acquire every grace, every truth, every light." With that fundamental lesson etched into her very existence—"I, nothing; God, All. I, non-being; God, Being"—Catherine passed from glory to glory in the life of the spirit so that she could have very well cried out with the Apostle St. Paul that it was no longer herself but Christ who lived.

Catherine's greatness lay in her deep humility. Her life-style and words were in themselves a bitter reproach to those who sought to minimize Christianity. She was understood by very few, parents and relatives included.

At the age of sixteen, after a hard and bitter struggle, Catherine was permitted to receive the white habit of the Third Order of St. Dominic. Although she took the vows of poverty, chastity and obedience, she remained at home with her family and carried out an unceasing apostolate of kindness and charity toward everyone: the poor, the sick, the imprisoned, those who loved and understood her and those who did not. Her living quarters consisted of one narrow room directly above the kitchen. It was furnished to her own taste with a long, wooden bench, which served as a seat during the day and a bed at night, and a small chest in which she kept her few meager belongings along with her instruments of penance: sackcloth, chains and scourges.

Catherine always kept before her the thought of Jesus scourged and bleeding, and she wanted to imitate Him by offering up pains and sufferings for the salvation of sinners. Summer and winter, day and night, she wore coarse, woolen garments. Her sleep was reduced to a bare minimum, if we can call it that—one half hour every other night. She never ate meat and she drank no wine. Her food consisted of a few vegetables. This manner of living was called "inhuman" by many. They considered Catherine a mad woman and a fanatic.

"O eternal God, receive the sacrifice of my life for the sake of this mystical body of holy Church."

But the human side in Catherine of Siena shone out no less brilliantly than the supernatural. Her life was a perfect blend of contemplation and action.

She was a woman in whom femininity, made immaculate by grace, stirred up in others a desire for purity. Her penances, mortification and ecstasies did not give her an appearance of severity or aloofness. On the contrary, she had a ready and spontaneous smile for everyone. She loved children and was fond of flowers. Singing delighted her and she thoroughly enjoyed creative poetry.

Catherine's extreme sense of practicality is obvious in the following humorous episode. Catherine's tremendous desire for sacrifice had driven her to great lengths, and she had devised a new method of mortification by acquiring and wearing a long hairshirt. Pleased with her new idea, she wore the scratchy garment day and night. Then as suddenly as she had begun wearing it, she disposed of it and it was seen no more. Her followers, who were curious about this abrupt change of attitude, questioned Sister Catherine. She replied that she had found hairshirts to be quite unhygienic and felt safer wearing iron chains about her body instead. Catherine's womanliness and logic could not be underestimated.

The year 1369 found the world in the midst of political convulsions. Wars, insurrections, and epidemics raged everywhere.

It was into just this world that Christ sent twenty-two-year-old Catherine, as a messenger of reconciliation and peace. In response to strong protests that she, a poor, weak woman, could do very little among wise noblemen, the Savior expressly commanded her: "Forget about your sex." He then proceeded to outline for her a man's program of action, which she followed "manfully" until the day of her death.

With God's grace nothing was impossible: the arms of war were literally thrown down at her feet. She cried out, "I have come only to gain souls, to snatch them from the hands of the demon."

Catherine waged this massive campaign for ten years, until death claimed her worn and exhausted body. She helped draw up terms of peace between the faction-torn cities of Italy. Invited or not, she acted as counselor to dukes, kings and emperors. Her fearlessness and courage shocked them into silence and obedience.

But her greatest accomplishment was the return of the Papacy from Avignon to Rome, where the Pope, as successor of St. Peter, rightfully belonged. It was for this above all that Catherine prayed, pleaded, wrote, spoke and mortified her already weakened body.

Just as Christ had come on earth to enkindle fire, so Catherine declared: "My nature is fire." It was a fire that burned fiercely, but did not consume. She felt herself one with the same God who spoke to Moses from the bush that burned but was not consumed. She wrote to her followers: "I am the fire; you are the sparks. Rise up, then, manfully! Do not await the right time, for time will not wait for you. Peace, peace, peace, for the love of God."

Yes, time was short for Catherine; ten years after she was called to her mission she was called to her eternal reward. At noon on April 29, 1380, Catherine of Siena lay dying. Slowly and painfully she lifted her head from her bed and whispered in a voice just audible to those standing at her bedside: "Father, into Your hands I commend my spirit."

Then she fell back on her pillow and closed her eyes in death. She was thirty-three years old.

Shortly before that final moment Catherine had managed to gasp: "I am going now...thanks be to our Savior...You, O Lord, are calling me and I am coming to You."

The happiest moment of Catherine's life had come. Like the prudent virgins of the Gospels, she went forth to meet her bridegroom: Christ the Lord.

2

all
people,
my
people

The setting sun silhouetted a strange little caravan approaching a small Breton town. The guards looked out across the plain and shouted a warning from the ramparts. The reply came back: "Master Vincent requests your hospitality."

Master Vincent! Who did not know Master Vincent? The rampart was abandoned in a matter of minutes, and the whole town turned out for a joyous welcome.

Master Vincent Ferrer was a bent old man. His black and white robe was tattered and worn, and his faithful donkey looked as if he could not walk another mile. Yet, somehow, both managed to survive their long and fatiguing travels.

What had just occurred at the gate of this Breton town had happened hundreds, perhaps thousands, of times in cities, towns and villages throughout France, Spain, Portugal and northern Italy.

Vincent Ferrer was born in Valencia, Spain, on January 23, 1350. At seventeen, he entered the Dominican Order and began his studies for the priesthood.

Those who knew him only in his later years would have been astounded by the appearance of the youthful Vincent. He was tall, broad and well-proportioned. His hair was light and his skin clear. His facial features were enhanced by dark, piercing eyes, which always gave the impression that he saw beyond external appearances, deep into the soul of the person before him. He was at once a man of understanding and zeal, mercy and fire. Everything in him was dominated by love of God and his life was completely permeated with prayer.

St. Augustine once classified prayer as: "Man's strength and God's weakness." It was this powerful prayer, confident and full of faith, which characterized Vincent, even from his youth. There wasn't a thing in his life that he could and did accomplish without prayer.

Vincent was as intelligent as he was holy. By the time he reached twenty-five, he was lecturing in the material sciences at Barcelona. After a brief study of Hebrew and Sacred Scripture, he received his master's degree in theology.

A few years later he launched the work that was to claim the greatest part of his life—preaching. That was Vincent's vocation and it was the reason why he had joined the Order of Preachers.

Wherever Vincent went, astonishing things began to happen. His sermons worked spiritual wonders. There were massive conversions from lives of sin and tepidity to lives of penance and fervor. Other signs accompanied his words. He cured the sick; he brought the dead back to life. Vincent spoke in his native dialect, but whoever heard him speak, heard him in his own tongue.

When Christ worked great wonders and signs, the apostles marveled. It was then that the Master told them He would· enable His followers, too, to work such signs. Vincent Ferrer was an apostle, and the wonders he worked were those prophesied by the Lord.

Vincent excelled in a very singular characteristic not often found in the men of his era. Brotherhood and unity were his favorite preaching topics. He not only preached them, but he lived them. Vincent tore down geographical barriers as he crossed and re-crossed boundaries in a rather disorderly fashion, making it clear to his followers that race, nationality and creed made no difference to him as long as there were people to evangelize.

In rain and sunshine, his little band trudged along over muddy or sun-parched roads. Perched atop his little donkey, Vincent felt his bare feet cut and bruised by the wooden stirrups attached to the saddle by heavy cords.

Morning came very early for him. He rose at 2:00 A.M. for prayer and meditation and the penitential practices he inflicted on his overworked body. This lasted until about 6:00 A.M., when he celebrated Mass. Then he took up a tiring round of preaching, visiting the sick, spiritual counseling, and mediation between parties and families at odds with each other. In crowds he was pushed, jostled, and imposed upon for endless favors, but his kindness and understanding never wore thin.

Vincent ate only one meal a day: soup, a tiny piece of fish and a glass of wine liberally mixed with water. Late into the evening after everyone else retired, he would again pray and meditate, then prepare the next day's sermons and take care of his mail. When he finally finished, he, too, retired, only to rouse himself from slumber soon after, at 2:00 A.M., to take up the round of the next day's activities. This was his daily routine for over twenty years.

Frequently, Vincent was misunderstood, criticized and even calumniated. But he cared little what others thought or said about him as long as the Gospel could be preached. Like St. Paul, he had reached the point of self-annihilation when only the Person of Jesus the Good Master radiated from his being.

In July of the year 1417, while preaching in the French city of Besançon, he visited a monastery of Poor Clare Nuns. There he met St. Collette, who prophesied that his death was two years away.

"In Spain?" he asked.

"No," she replied, "in France."

Vincent made an act of resignation to God's will. He had served the Divine Master faithfully during life, cost what it might; he would serve Him to the very end.

As prophesied, two years later, at the age of sixty-nine, Vincent Ferrer lay on his deathbed in the small city of Vannes in Brittany far from his native Spain, and far from his Dominican priory. But he was not far from people who showed great affection for him. Even here in northern France, he found friends who cared for him and loved him. They crowded around him, vying with one another in an effort to show him every kindness. To this show of anxiety and attention, he responded calmly: "In ten days I shall die." Faithful to his word, on April 5, 1419, Vincent went to his eternal reward.

The theme of Vincent's preaching and the work of his life had been unity. As he waited for the final summons, Vincent had the grace of knowing that the Council of Constance, which had been recently convoked, was drawing the Christian world together in a bond of brotherly love.

He closed his eyes in peace with the realization that his works, prayers and sacrifices had not been in vain. All were bearing fruit.

Like Isaiah of old, Vincent had heard the word of the Lord:

" Whom shall I send? Who will go for us? " (Is. 6:8)

He had responded: "Here I am...send me" (*Ibid.*).

3

child
of
God

It was December 23, 1430.

The English-held city of Rouen presented itself for the first time to the young French maiden, Joan of Arc. Fear and uncertainty clutched at her heart as she was rudely dragged through the streets and mocked from all sides by a menacing crowd of onlookers. There were no looks of sympathy for the Maid of Orleans, whom her own king had not attempted to rescue from enemy hands.

The procession suddenly came to an abrupt halt. One of the guards shouted: "There, you witch! Look up there! That's your new home. You'll stay there until you admit that you never really heard any voices." A formidable grey castle loomed high in the distance. Its towers cast long shadows over the entire city. Joan shuddered at the sight. But there was no escape. Joan knew that her voices had already told her she would die, and die soon.

When the procession reached the castle entrance, Joan cast one last look out across the horizon toward Domremy.... There her mother and father were thinking of her and praying for her. She was certain of that. But did they know yet about this terrible turn of events? Did they know that the Burgundians had sold her to the English? All these thoughts raced through her mind and stopped cold in the face of the inevitable: She was now a prisoner of the English. She would never regain freedom. She would die.

"And do you know how a witch dies?" The Earl of Warwick's question still rang in her ears. "By fire."

Heart in her throat, she could still hear her own gasping, startled reply: "Fire?"

"Yes, fire. Now we'll see how long you'll continue this foolishness. Your trial is scheduled for February 21. Until then you will reside at the castle of Rouen. Now, witch, get out of here. The English soldiers are waiting for you. They are all very anxious to see the pretty young maiden that cost them so dearly. You mean a lot to them. Remember, they paid no small price for you. Now, get out."

The castle in which Joan was to reside, as the Earl of Warwick had so carefully phrased it, was nothing more than a dark, damp prison. Her room was nothing more than a dungeon. The guards escorted her to this cell, threw her on a bed and chained her wrists and ankles to the four bedposts.

The stark realities of prison life were a horrifying experience for Joan. A mere teenager, comely in appearance, as pure as an angel and kind and compassionate to everyone, even her persecutors, she was roughly mistreated and beaten. Yet never once did she succumb to the taunts and rude advances of these rough men. Her only love was Christ, and to Him she was faithful to the end. Her only consolation was the joy of knowing that she was suffering for her Savior, who had once suffered for her.

There was plenty of time to think. Joan traced and retraced the events that had reduced her to this condition. She never regretted one moment of them: Her early years in Domremy...the first time she heard the voices of St. Michael, St. Catherine and St. Margaret...the insistent commands of these saints concerning the mission she was to carry out...the difficulties of the beginnings, the scorn, the ridicule, the hardships of camp life, the repugnance of battle, her nausea at the sight of blood, the hard-won victories, the coronation of the Dauphin, his sudden change of attitude toward her, her capture by the Burgundians, the king's refusal to ransom her, and now the last lap of her journey to Rouen.

It had all been so hard to believe. Yet Joan knew that God was leading her and that His ways are often mysterious. All she need do was follow. He would guide her and protect her. When the time came, He would tell her what she should say.

The weeks passed—nights and days of fear and anxiety, alleviated only by fleeting consolations that followed fervent prayer, for her trust in God could come only from Him.

When February 21 arrived, it was a worn and haggard Joan that confronted the stern faces of her accusers. The verdict was a foregone conclusion— everyone knew that—but it must be made to look good in front of those whose consciences were what her accusers might call "overly scrupulous."

And so it began — three long months of torture for that poor peasant girl, who knew neither how to read nor write. If only they could discredit her as a heretic, thought her accusers. If only they could make her say her voices were a fraud! But no matter how cunningly they phrased their questions or in what manner they tried to confuse her, Joan's answers were clear and straightforward. The accusers were foiled by this wisp of a girl who backed down before no man. Their defeat at the hands of the young peasant drove them to exasperation.

"Admit that your voices were a hoax!"

"Admit it was a lie!"

"Confess that you practice witchcraft and your success comes from the devil!"

Joan's once sparkling eyes were bloodshot and tired. Her body had been reduced to a skeleton. Her physical stamina had been alarmingly weakened by tortures, but her will power and convictions were stronger than ever. Her voices still spoke to her and encouraged her to carry on with fortitude.

The final statement of the Maid of Orleans was categorical: "God *has* truly sent me and my voices *are* from Him." The verdict was delivered: Guilty. Joan's days were numbered.

On Tuesday, May 29, 1431, Joan of Arc was led to her execution. Hailed by her heavenly voices as Maid of France and Child of God, she was to be burned as a heretic and a witch by her human accusers. Joan was bound to the stake, and the fire was lit. As the flames rose higher and higher, the girl kept her gaze fixed on a crucifix held before her eyes by a priest who had compassion on her in her last moments. "Jesus, Jesus," she whispered, "Jesus, Jesus."

Suddenly the onlookers began to realize what an awful crime was being committed. "We are burning

"Blest are those persecuted for holiness' sake; the reign of God is theirs."

Matthew 5:10

a saint!" But it was already too late. Joan's pure soul had winged its way to heaven.

The first streaks of dawn found Jacques d'Arc pacing back and forth feverishly. His wife called to him gently. "Please get some sleep. I know you're worried about Joan. Trust in God. He will take care of her. He will bring her home again. They can't kill her—she's just a child."

For several weeks Jacques had withheld the sad news from his wife, but he knew he couldn't carry his burden much longer. He continued to pace and to watch the steady climb of the sun.

"Eat some breakfast," Joan's mother urged, "and get out into the fields and take your mind off her."

Jacques knew from the sun that it was now eight o'clock. He couldn't hold back his sorrow any longer.

"Mama, there's something I've got to tell you. It's going to hurt you very much, but God will help us bear this sorrow.... Joan has been condemned to death. She is dying right now, this morning."

The woman clutched her husband's hand. Weakly she asked: "How is she dying?"

"Oh, Mama," sobbed Joan's father, "I can't answer that. Please don't ask me."

"Papa, how is Joan dying?"

"By fire..." his voice broke off.

Mama d'Arc fell to her knees on the bare wooden floor: "O Jesus, she was always so afraid of fire. Please take away the pain and fear.... Oh God, not by fire, not by fire...."

"Mama," said Jacques gently, "if our daughter was so pure and holy here on earth, so obedient and loving, certainly she is already enjoying the reward she so well deserved."

And as the May sun continued its climb upward, they suddenly felt that their Joan was very near them and would always remain so.

3. Moments of Decision

4

saint
of
the
impossible

Far from the tumult of large and crowded cities, perched high on the sunbathed mountains of Umbria, sits the peaceful and pleasant town of Cascia. This village is so small and insignificant that it would be unknown to the rest of humanity were it not for one of its citizens—a woman who came from the outlying district of Rocca Porena, a mere cluster of houses, sheltering about one hundred inhabitants.

Rita of Cascia was born in the year 1381. All Italy was rife with wars, violence and indecency, but to Anthony and Amata Mancini, Rita brought nothing but peace and serenity. If we believe in the power of prayer and the omnipotence of God's grace, then we can readily accept the fact that Rita was born to this holy and God-fearing couple when they were well advanced in years.

As Rita grew in age, she also grew in virtues — in those virtues that easily attract the love and appreciation of others. Rocca Porena could boast of no schools, but Rita learned much wisdom and knowledge from a deep study of her favorite "book," the crucifix. Aware of it or not, she was following the admonition of St. Paul to have knowledge of Christ alone—the crucified Christ.

Rita's greatest desire was to serve God and consecrate every fiber of her being to Him alone behind the walls of a religious monastery. But God's ways are not always ours. Pious and good as they were, her parents, according to the customs of their times, promised her in marriage. Her husband-to-be was a rough and insolent young man from a neighboring district. Rita had no other choice but to obey her parents' wishes. Otherwise she would have incurred the wrathful vengeance of Paul Di Fernando, who would have stopped at nothing in order to have her as his bride.

From the beginning, her married life was marked by the cross. At every turn, Rita met with abuse, curses, insults and hate. From day to day she lived in constant fear that her husband's wild ways would result in his being carried home dead or that he might be arrested for manslaughter or some other crime. His repentance and return to God were the only things she desired.

Rita bore Paul's cruel beatings and maltreatment heroically, without a word of impatience. Gradually, her prayers, fastings and other sacrifices, along with her example of meekness and kindness, led her husband to recognize his wrongs. One evening he came home, threw himself down at her feet and with tears of sorrow begged her forgiveness.

Taking along her two sons, James and Paul, Rita frequently went to visit the poor of the area and serve their needs as best she could, for she was very poor herself. After his conversion, her husband readily approved of this charity. He deeply admired the woman who had remained true to him in spite of his shortcomings and failures, the woman who had loved him even though it could have cost her her life.

This more happy period of Rita's life soon ended abruptly.

One day, when her husband was returning from business in a nearby town, he was suddenly attacked and murdered by a vengeful assassin.

Overcoming her shock and horror, Rita hurried to the scene of the slaughter and claimed the body of her poor husband. She prayed and fasted unceasingly for the repose of his soul.

Shortly thereafter, Rita began to detect a change in her two sons. They were planning and preparing to avenge their father's murder. Nothing could have been farther from the mind of Rita, who had already forgiven the assassin. Rita heroically implored God with prayers and tears to take the lives of her sons rather than let them commit such a terrible crime. To her, the salvation of their immortal souls was much more important than their bodily life.

Within a short time both of them fell ill. Rita procured every remedy she could to save their lives, but to no avail. Both died barely a year after their father's death.

Humanly speaking, Rita was now completely alone in the world; all family ties had been broken.

A few months after her sons' deaths, Rita knocked on the door of Cascia's Augustinian convent and presented herself to the Mother Superior, asking admission. However, the community accepted only young, unmarried women and Rita's request was flatly refused.

Although there were other convents in Cascia, Rita kept returning to the Augustinians as if by instinct. As often as she returned, she was refused. Then, one night while she was praying, she heard a voice call her by name. She looked around and saw no one. After a few seconds she again heard the same call: "Rita, Rita." Puzzled, Rita got up and went outside. Suddenly she found herself in the convent chapel of the Augustinian Nuns. That door which had been closed in her face, that door which had been so firmly bolted for the night, had miraculously opened to admit her. The next morning, after combing the convent for signs of a break-in, the amazed nuns agreed to let Rita stay.

Rita turned out to be more than suited to their type of life. She was already well advanced in the way of perfection. She received the religious habit and was soon permitted to take the vows of poverty, chastity and obedience.

Rita now entered the last and most painful period of her life. Wed as she was to Christ, she begged Him for a share in His own passion. Only thus, she felt, could she really become one with her divine Bridegroom in a union more binding than any earthly marriage. And Christ granted the final desire of this selfless woman. One day while she was at prayer, Rita fixed her gaze on the crucifix. She felt an acute pain penetrate her forehead. A gaping, festering wound appeared. Christ then revealed to her that she would suffer the pain of wearing a mystical crown of thorns until the day of her death. To add to her misery, the wound became putrid and repulsive, and her sisters in religion shunned her for fear of contagion.

For fifteen years, Rita underwent this terrible humiliation. Her only comfort lay in the words Christ had spoken to her: "If you liken yourself to me in your sufferings, then it will inevitably result—in accord with the doctrine of my Apostle Paul—that you will be like me also in grace and in glory."

Rita's final illness lasted three years; then, on May 22, 1457, her beautiful soul winged its way toward heaven.

The moment Rita died, the convent bell began to ring without anyone touching it. The room where she lay glowed with a heavenly light, and her face became fresh and youthful. Although St. Rita of Cascia was never embalmed, her body still lies incorrupt in the chapel of the convent in Cascia. The wound in her forehead is completely healed. At various times, throughout the years since her death nearly seven centuries ago, numerous witnesses have testified to the fact that her body moves. Many other miracles have taken place at her coffin. Thus she is now called the *saint of the impossible,* and indeed in her own life she found that with God, all things are possible.

5

a call
to obedience
and
suffering

The year was 1396. Twelve-year-old Frances Bussi stood as still as a stone. Her father's eyes flashed with authority; his icy words stung: "Frances, you are my daughter and as such you are to do as I say. It has already been arranged, and I won't hear another word."

Frances swallowed hard and bit her lip. She was a child of her age and that meant her parents had the right to arrange for her marriage without consulting her. Her childhood was coming to an abrupt halt as womanhood's heavy responsibilities fell on her young shoulders.

After her parents left the room, Frances had a good cry and went to look for the head maid. Together they went to see Frances' confessor. When Frances had made her tearful plea, the priest counseled her, "My child, to obey and to suffer is your vocation. You are to become a saint by leading the life of an exemplary Christian wife and mother. Are you crying because you're doing God's will or because you want God to do your will?... I give you my blessing." Resigned, Frances composed herself and calmly returned home.

Frances married Lorenzo Ponziani, a very wealthy, kind, refined young man. At the sumptuous wedding feast, the young bride enthralled her guests with her beauty, serenity and graciousness. Frances gave no indication of her internal struggle. Doing God's will did not lessen the pain that tore at her heart, but did make it bearable. The endless stream of parties and dining that accompanied the week's festivities went along smoothly. The entire Ponziani family was delighted with Frances and loaded her with one gift after another.

But the tremendous effort Frances made and the new social pressures proved too much for her. She fell deathly ill. Almost completely paralyzed and unable to talk, Frances lay feverish and bedridden for a full year. Her father was beside himself with grief. He blamed himself for being too harsh and almost violent in forcing Frances to submit to his will.

One night as Frances lay immovable, a bright light filled her lonely room. She blinked in amazement as a radiant young man stood by her bedside.

"My name is St. Alexius. God has sent me to you to ask you if you wish to get well."

Frances hesitated a moment. Oh, it would be so much easier to die, to escape from the dreadful, uncertain future. But then, she mustn't anticipate God's will. Firmly, she responded, "As God wants."

"Then you shall get well and give great glory to God with your life." With that, he touched her with his cloak and disappeared.

Imagine the shock and joy that filled the household the next morning when Frances walked down to breakfast, completely cured!

Lorenzo, who already greatly admired the spiritual qualities of his child-bride, was filled with even greater awe and reverence for her after her miraculous cure. Clearly, his wife was exceptionally beloved of God. He was grateful God had joined their lives in matrimony. With deep love and mutual respect, Lorenzo and Frances fulfilled their marital obligations and experienced the strength of the graces received in the sacrament. In the forty years they were married they were never known to have an argument. God blessed their union with six children, the first three of whom died in infancy. Then a son, Battista, was born, followed by a second son, Evangelista, and a daughter, Agnes.

About two years after the birth of Battista, Cecilia, Frances' much loved mother-in-law, passed away. Her father-in-law, her brother-in-law, Paul, and Paul's wife, Vanezza, all agreed that the full responsibility for the household should now fall upon Frances. With tact, firmness, and kindness joined to an almost inexhaustible supply of energy, Frances began to manage the house, the servants, the buying and distribution of goods and the frequent balls and banquets that their family's social standing demanded. The Ponziani Palace held a prominent place in wealthy, medieval Roman society. With simplicity and womanly dedication, Frances and Vanezza accomplished what was expected of them as charming and gracious hostesses.

Apparently completely submerged in the luxury and pomp of high society, how was Frances to become a saint? Every free moment she could find, Frances would go to her oratory to pray. Then she devised various ways and means of sacrificing herself. These she concealed carefully from the eyes of all, except Vanezza, who shared her secrets of mortification and joined her in their practice. Hidden beneath their gorgeous velvet, jewel-bedecked gowns, the two holy women wore irritating hair shirts. But it was obedience above all that held first place: obedience to their husbands and service and love to their children and household.

After Frances had personally attended to the early instruction of her children, she asked Lorenzo's permission to expand her sphere of action. Lorenzo and Paul gave Frances and Vanezza permission to visit the poor and sick of the city. These two youthful noblewomen became a familiar sight to the people of Rome. Like angels of mercy, they traversed the overcrowded streets, distributing alms, in hovels and hospitals, in Christ's name.

Then, grave trials, permitted by God, tore the peaceful and tranquil Ponziani family asunder. Rome and the world shook violently from the storm of the Great Western Schism. Wars and insurrections gripped entire cities and regions.

One frightful day, Frances' blood froze and her throat tightened as a stretcher carrying her beloved Lorenzo was laid at her feet. Lorenzo had received a severe knife wound right below his heart. Frances laid her head on Lorenzo's chest and heard a feeble heart beat. With trembling fingers she tore away the shirt, and cried out to some servants to fetch water and clean linens, and others to find a priest and a doctor. Meanwhile she whispered acts of love of God into Lorenzo's ears, and prayed God to spare him.

Long, fatiguing, love-filled weeks of nursing, praying and watching gradually brought Lorenzo back to health.

But sorrow soon struck again. Paul was taken prisoner by a political enemy and would be killed unless nine-year-old Battista were given over as a hostage.

After asking God's will in prayer, Frances courageously brought her son to the enemy, the Count of Traja. She then ran into a nearby church, flung herself at the foot of the altar and poured out her maternal grief. She prayed and prayed. How long she remained there she didn't know. All of a sudden two small arms swung around her neck as a frightened little boy cried, "Mommy!" Tousling Battista's sandy hair, Frances questioned him as to how he had escaped.

He answered, "Those men put me on a horse, but the horse wouldn't move. So they put me on four others and they didn't move either. The men looked real scared then. They told me to go away because they didn't want to fool around with 'strange' powers. You must have prayed real hard, Mommy! I'm sure glad to be back." Eyes brimming with tears of gratitude, Frances hugged her son and thanked God. Because Frances had complied with the Count's demands, her brother-in-law's life was spared.

A year later, Paul was still in prison when another invasion of Rome took place. This time, both Lorenzo and Battista had to flee into exile. Evangelista and Agnes safely hidden in a secret hallway, Vanezza and Frances clung frantically to one another as wild, drunken soldiers, searching for Lorenzo, rammed in the palace door and smashed everything in sight. Frances suppressed the resentment that rose in her heart and prayed for the grace to forgive the unjust aggressors.

Then, patiently, with no men to help them, the two young women began to clear away the rubble. When the dining hall was finally cleared out, Frances converted it into a hospital. To add to the horrors and sufferings of war, there were widespread famine and pestilence. Barely six months apart, Evangelista and Agnes went to heaven, little victims of the plague.

Frances, the valiant woman, wiped away fresh tears and set to work to alleviate the sorrows of hundreds of others who needed comfort, words of faith, and tender care. For seven years, she and Vanezza continued their works of charity, prayers, and penance. They were joined by other young matrons, inspired to imitate their generosity and charity. All the while Frances' heart ached because of the uncertainty of Battista's and Lorenzo's safety.

Finally the day arrived when Paul, Battista and Lorenzo returned home. Paul had suffered a nervous breakdown. Young Battista was in good spirits, but his father staggered into the palace haggard and worn. Lorenzo became even more depressed and disconsolate when he learned of the death of his two younger children. Lorenzo looked at Frances long and hard. He saw how pale and emaciated she was. Lorenzo had known Frances as no one else had. He had seen her when her proud spirit had resented the wrongs and injustices of her times. He had seen her when she had fought to overcome her impetuosity, her obstinacy and her other faults. And he had followed her examples of holiness, meekness and humility. She would help him now.

In the months that followed, Frances was always at Lorenzo's side, nursing him with untiring tenderness. One night as she eased him back on his pillow, Lorenzo took her hand gently and whispered, "In your love God has given me so much!" He had bid farewell, dying in the arms of his saintly wife.

Shortly after Lorenzo's death, Frances buried Paul and Vanezza.

Battista had meanwhile married happily and was settled. Frances made known her decision to end her days as a nun in the order of Oblates she had founded a few years before. Overcoming the tears and protests of her son and daughter-in-law, Frances entered the convent on the feast of St. Benedict. For four more years, she continued a life of strictest penance and mortification. Then God called her home, where every tear is wiped away, to receive her reward. Frances of Rome leaves every wife and mother a shining example of domestic virtues. Her life eloquently testifies to the fact that a person becomes a saint by doing God's will in the station and condition of life into which God's providence has led him. Of encouragement to wives and mothers who wish they had more time for prayer or meditation is a statement Frances of Rome made, "It is praiseworthy for a married woman to be devout, but she must never forget that she is a housewife. And sometimes she must leave God at prayer to find Him in her housekeeping."

6

trial
for
life

A great hushed crowd had gathered to see him leave the courtroom. Whispers of "guilty," "death" filtered through the lines. Hands reached out; voices were raised to promise prayers, to thank, to encourage, to cry. Sir Thomas More turned all his attention to the mere accomplishment of walking, something very difficult in his weakened condition. He followed the guards along the familiar route back to the tower.

From the throng a voice cried out above all the others: "Dad, oh, Dad!" Meg rushed forward to cling to her father, her confidant, her inspiration. She could not see his face through her tears. She clung to him with such strength he could not move on. He took her face in both hands and gazed once more on the loved symbol of his whole family. Could he leave them? All his life had been lived for them. They were God's gift to him and he had always tried to be a worthy husband and father. Could he leave them now to the mercy of the king? No, no! But he *could* leave them to the mercy of God, from whom all fatherhood on earth takes its name. Lightning-like, one thought crowded in upon another. The guards were urging, pushing him to move on. This was the trial far more fearful than any man's tribunal. But God never permits us to be tempted beyond our strength.

"Meg," he whispered quickly, "whatever I suffer is God's will. Do you believe that, Meg?"

Surely he saw the answer written in her eyes before he gave his blessing and moved on toward the prison. If he hadn't seen it then, he knew it, when a second time Meg broke out of the crowd, pushed her way between guards and kissed her father, so that later he wrote to her, "I never loved you more than when you kissed me last."

Yes, Meg believed. Meg understood. And not even Lady Alice could fail to understand when Sir Thomas spoke his last words as he stood upon the scaffold: "I die the King's good servant, but God's first."

Father and son teams are certainly nothing new in the long history of men. In sixteenth-century England a father and son were among the most loved and trusted lawyers of their day. Even today Thomas More, known then as the Young More, is the venerated patron of lawyers, a model man of principle whose uncompromising determination led him to death and opened the door to life.

Unless his law practice took him out of town, a day never passed that the young lawyer More did not kneel before the older More for his blessing. Even as Lord Chancellor of England he did not consider it below his station to ask his father's blessing, counsel and advice in public or private.

Perhaps this close, affectionate relationship with his father explains St. Thomas More's delight in his own family life. Nothing pleased him more than an evening full of rollicking fun with his wife and four children, followed by a quiet time of conversation, storytelling and prayer.

Theirs was a family of love. Only God could see the cloud which was soon to cover the happy group. When little Meg was five years old, and baby John near his first birthday, the sweet-natured wife of Sir Thomas died. It was a shock and sorrow that this man would carry for the rest of his life. On her tombstone he had written: "Dear Jane, Thomas More's little wife."

There would never be another Jane in his life — the love of his youth, the one who shared his most secret dreams. His second wife, the Lady Alice, was practical, staunchly loyal, really kind in her own sort of way. She was not his dear Jane, yet she won his grateful affection for the excellent upbringing she gave to his children. She was reserved in her manner, but generous in her devotion to her family. Soon enough they found it not hard to call her wife and mother.

Thomas More was a lawyer by desire and profession. When he was called to the king's service, he would have relished the opportunities it would give his lawyer's skill if it had not curtailed his family life. Life at King Henry's court was anything but upright and honest. Thomas More was a startling confrontation to many a conscience. His open, sincere nature fast became known not only to the king, but to the entire court as well.

The youthful king was delighted with the wit and sparkle lent to the conversation by Sir Thomas. It got so bad — in fact, Sir Thomas saw his family so little — that he decided to try his best to become "dull" so as not to be so much in demand. He did

eventually get called upon less because Henry
realized he was a family man, but Thomas More never
did succeed in becoming a bore.

Sir Thomas' reputation for honest justice became
a tradition among the poor commoners. The story is
told of an old beggar lady who came to the courtroom
and complained that her little dog had run away and
been taken in by a wealthy lady. The poor soul
lamented that whenever she tried to get the dog back,
the servants refused to let her see the lady of the
house.

"Well, just who is this good woman?" More
asked. "Perhaps they will let me see her."

"She is the wife of the Lord Chancellor," the
lady smiled sweetly.

Sir Thomas sent for his wife. Lady Alice and the
dog appeared shortly. At one end of the courtroom
stood Lady Alice. At the other, the beggar lady
waited. The Lord Chancellor walked to the center
of the room with the little dog wiggling in his arms.

"Now, whomever the dog goes to may keep it."
The little puppy, set on the floor, dashed toward the
old woman.

"It is yours," Sir Thomas said cheerfully.

The old woman was so amazed at his kindness
that she made a gift of the dog to Lady Alice.

The kindness of Sir Thomas was not reserved
for the needy poor who constantly sought his help.
It was extended first to his own family. His cares
were many; his worries were those of a nation, yet
he never aired his problems at home. Only to his
oldest child, his beloved Meg, did he sometimes
confide his hopes and fears.

Of all his sufferings, perhaps the most acute was
not the prison confinement, nor the interminable

questionings, nor the humiliation of being tried in a court of friends, but that those dearest to his heart, his family, could scarce understand his reason for dying.

He didn't really expect Lady Alice to agree with his point of view on the king's marriage. He loved her practical ways, her efficient management of the household. What the king did neither concerned nor worried her. But what *Thomas* did never went unnoticed. He tried his best to explain to her why it was impossible for him to sign the Act of Supremacy. She admired his virtue, but could not understand his holy stubbornness in refusing to act by man's standards rather than God's.

It was Meg who brought the most sorrow, as she had also brought the most joy, to his fatherly heart. Few visitors were allowed Sir Thomas in prison. Meg, however, was allowed in more frequently than anyone else. The first time she actually saw her father behind bars and realized the seriousness of the situation, she cried and begged, really begged, her father to sign the Act which declared King Henry VIII supreme head of the Church of England. Words, usually at his instant command, were lacking to him. He had so much to say, but all his efforts reached only as far as his lips and there froze in icy silence. Only after she left did he break, and muffled sobs filled the cell.

His pen dipped into his soul as he wrote to Meg: "None of the terrible things that might happen to me touched me so grievously as to see you, my well-beloved child, in such piteous manner, labor to persuade me about the thing which I have of pure necessity, for respect for my own soul, often given you so precise an answer."

He was a lawyer, but not a judge of other men's souls. He never questioned the integrity of those who did sign the Act. "They have their conscience," he would repeat. "I have mine."

It broke his heart when his family pleaded with him to give in and come home. His answer was always the same, a gentle yet firm "no." He held no grudge with any man; he had no reason to fear man's judgment seat, or God's. He had learned to pray from his own devout father and it was to prayer that he turned night and day. God alone was his source of consolation, of much-needed strength to bear the trial which awaited him.

With a conscience at peace with man and God, he faced his judges and received their sentence as though from friends. Slowly, solemnly it was pronounced—"Guilty...death!"

"I forgive you," replied the defendant with a sincerity which moved every man in court. "I forgive you as Stephen forgave Saul. And just as now both are holy saints in heaven and shall continue there friends together forever, so I trust and pray that, though Your Lordships have been on earth my judges of condemnation, we may meet hereafter merrily together in heaven."

Sir Thomas accepted his death sentence with such cheerfulness, it is surprising to know to what degree he really feared it. He admitted to Meg that his fear of death was far greater than it should be for a Christian. But by the grace of God, his natural fear of death remained concealed beneath his sparkling wit.

As he stood on the hateful scaffold ready for execution, a joke sprang uninvited to his lips. He chided the executioner to do his job well lest he lose his reputation, then placed his neck upon the block. To the astonishment of all, he stopped the executioner with a sudden exclamation. And drawing aside his beard so that it might escape the axe, Sir Thomas said, "Spare this, for it has committed no treason."

"I die the King's
good servant,
but God's first."

St. Thomas More—beloved husband, father, martyr for the Faith—has rightly been called a man for all seasons. God tried him and found him worthy of Himself.

The Holy Bible says:

"Happy the man whose conscience does not reproach him,

　　who has not lost hope" (Sir. 14:2).

"When God, in the beginning, created man,

　　he made him subject to his own free choice.

If you choose you can keep the commandments;

　　it is loyalty to do his will.

Before man are life and death,

　　whichever he chooses shall be given him"

　　　　(Sir. 15:14, 15, 17).

7

only
one
man

"Don't you all agree?" asked the king, certain to receive an affirmative answer. The spokesman for the bishops arose, "Yes," he said, "we will agree."

Henry VIII had appealed to Rome for a dispensation from his marriage with Catherine of Aragon. The Pope withheld a decision, hoping that the infatuation for Ann Boleyn would die, and with it, the marriage doubts. Henry, not one to accept delay, came to a drastic solution. The bishops of England were called together to declare the marriage of Catherine and Henry invalid. Henry spoke to them gently — persuading, entreating — it was a matter of conscience, he insisted.

A matter of conscience it was indeed for John Fisher, gathered with the other bishops in the assembly hall.

"No sir, not I! You have not *my* consent to it!" rang out a voice with startling firmness.

The entire assembly turned as one man to look at John Fisher, in whom fear of offending God replaced fear of Henry.

"Look at this," the infuriated king shouted, waving a parchment document. "Isn't this your signature and seal?"

"No sir, it is *not!* I said to you I never would consent to such an act, for it is against my conscience!"

The embarrassed spokesman admitted he had forged the seal. There was an awkward silence, then, "It doesn't matter anyway," Henry stated through clenched teeth. "We won't argue with you, for you are but one man."

"You are but one man"—yes, one man and his God.

In 1535, June in England was much as it is today. Warm, lazy days succeed each other with little difference. Only occasional summer storms and fogs break the monotony. But June 22nd of that year has been long remembered in London, and seldom mentioned.

For John Fisher, the Cardinal-Bishop of Rochester, it was the day of his martyrdom, the day of his glory, the day of his entrance into eternal life.

John Fisher grew up among the shops, fields and woods of a bustling medieval town. His hometown of Beverly was well known for its miracle and passion plays. It is not unlikely that John played parts in these dramas. On every major religious feast he and the other boys must have delighted in the crowds of tourists that invaded their village in order to see the famous plays.

Life was not all fun and joy, however. John's young life was tinged by sorrow at the death of his father. The eight-year-old boy, oldest of four children, was suddenly the man of the house. We can well imagine his childish voice taking an adult determination as he sought to console his mother. He slipped his small arm into hers and shouldered responsibilities far beyond his boyish capacity.

John Fisher was ordinary in many ways, but he had more than his share of intelligence. He was eager to know and quick to learn. His studies were completed at Cambridge, where we can assume he engaged in mischief as boys do today.

In June of 1491 came a day that alone could rival the glory of the day in June of 1535. It was the day of John's ordination to the priesthood. His priesthood was to lead him into the king's court as confessor and advisor, and as teacher of the future King Henry VIII.

His priestly life was crowned with the fullness of Holy Orders when in 1504 he was consecrated Bishop of Rochester. The diocese of Rochester was insignificant, the poorest in England, but for St. John Fisher it was the place and position given him by God's will, and that was enough for this energetic bishop, whose dignified bearing inspired respect and trust in all he met.

John Fisher had always been a man of uncompromising principles, a priest of decisive action, a bishop of prayerful dependence on the will of God.... And then the matter of the king's marriage came up.

Angered beyond reason when the annulment was not granted, Henry, in 1534, issued a document entitled "The Supremacy Act." He was henceforth to be considered the supreme head of the Church in England. Bishop John Fisher, along with Thomas More and others, refused to sign the Act. They were imprisoned immediately in the infamous Tower.

The prison conditions were inhuman enough to break the health of even the strongest of men. John Fisher, already worn out by age, sickness and untiring service to his flock, became so thin and pale that it seemed death would claim him before the court could condemn him. His humble plea for a blanket, warm clothes and sufficient food went unheeded.

His Holiness, Pope Paul III, raised his faithful bishop to the dignity of a cardinal, hoping this would help to save his life. Henry VIII had a ready reply when he heard of the appointment: "While I cannot permit a cardinal's hat to be brought to England," he wrote, "I will be glad to arrange for Fisher's head to be sent to Rome instead."

Henry still tried every means to persuade the cardinal to reverse his decision and sign the Act. Unsuccessful in his attempts, he tried to force an open verbal denial that the king was head of the Church in England. This would have made for an easy trial with condemnation as a matter of course.

An agent was sent by Henry to trick the cardinal into an outright denial. He made the cardinal believe that he was there confidentially and swore secrecy, saying it was only to relieve the king's conscience. But what was said in confidence was repeated in court, supplying sufficient material to convict the cardinal of high treason.

At another time several bishops visited the cardinal to try to persuade him to take the oath. The cardinal simply replied: "Seeing I am an old man and look not long to live, I do not intend (by the help of God) to trouble my conscience in pleasing the king in this way, whatever becomes of me; but rather, here to spend out the remnant of my old days in praying to God for him."

June 22, 1535, began at 5:00 A.M. for St. John Fisher. His jailor pushed open the huge door and gently awakened the loved prelate who lay on a cot in the dark, damp cell.

"It is the king's pleasure," he announced, "that you shall go to the block before noon."

"What time must be my hour to leave here?" asked the cardinal.

"About ten."

"Well, then," answered the cardinal, "let me sleep an hour or two, for I slept not much this night." And lest the jailor interpret this request as a sign of anxiety, the cardinal continued, "not for fear of death, I tell you, but because of my sickness and weakness."[1]

And with the peace of mind that comes only from a conscience pure in the sight of God, he went back to sleep to await his execution. Only after the sun had begun to scorch the summer air and announce the approach of noon, was John Fisher led to the scaffold. He ascended the scaffold stairs without help and stood straight and determined before the people he had served as a good shepherd. His lips continually moved in prayer as he prepared his soul for the moment for which we all live and die—to see God face to face and give an accounting of our days.

He blessed his executioner before speaking briefly to the crowd. "Christian people," he addressed them, "I am come here to die for the faith of Christ's Catholic Church. And I thank God...I have not feared death.... I desire you help me, and assist me with your prayers, that at the very point and instant of my death's stroke, and in the very moment of my death, I then faint not in any point of the Catholic faith for any fear. And I pray, God save the King...."[2] His voice resounded so distinctly that even those on the crowd's edge could hear each word.

1. Words of John Fisher taken from "St. John Fisher" by E.E. Reynolds, p. 281 (Kenedy, N.Y.).
2. Ibid.

Then he knelt and prayed a hymn of thanksgiving with such fervor that many onlookers joined in the prayer. All the vigor of bygone youthful days seemed to return to set his eyes flashing with a fire lit by God Himself.

Of his own accord he laid his neck upon the block and in an instant went to meet the God he had served unrelentingly, faithful unto death.

"You are but one man," St. John Fisher, one man who thought it far better to be a man approved by God than by the world. You are but one man who listened and took to heart the words of St. Paul, beheaded for the same Faith so many years before:

"Hold fast to faith and a good conscience. Some men, by rejecting the guidance of conscience, have made shipwreck of their faith" (1 Tm. 1:19). "I charge you to preach the word, to stay with this task whether convenient or inconvenient—correcting, reproving, appealing—constantly teaching and never losing patience" (2 Tm. 4:2). "You can depend on this: If we have died with him, we shall also live with him; if we hold out to the end we shall also reign with him" (2 Tm. 2:11-12).

8

a flame
without
smoke

The horse carefully picked his footing amid the stones, lurching now suddenly to the left, now to the right, to avoid slipping down the embankment. Inigo began to wonder about his decision to leave the main road to take to the mountain trails. He recalled the tales he had heard as a boy about robbers hidden along mountain paths, lying in wait for lone travelers. Maybe he shouldn't have come alone.

Suddenly his fears became reality! Two horses with heavily armed riders were approaching. A flick of the rein, a tap with his heel, and his own horse responded in a burst of energy. With no show of the fear that was fast filling his heart, Inigo rode straight by the two men. Maybe his poverty-stricken appearance would save him. He had hardly passed them by when he heard the beat of pursuing hooves. For the first time in his life, Ignatius of Loyola experienced real fear. How long could he stay in the lead? His horse had carried him many miles already. They were both exhausted. Then he made a decision that shows what true courage is made of. He pulled his mount to an abrupt stop, prayed to God for help, and turned to face the two men.

"I have no weapon but the help of God," he told them. "And I have no riches but the love of God. Gladly would I share these with you." He paused, waiting for whatever God would permit to happen.

The two men smiled broadly, then burst into uncontrolled laughter when they realized what had happened.

"Inigo," they managed to get out, "we are employed by your brother, Don Martin, to come look for you and escort you *safely* home. We aren't cutthroats, but we wouldn't mind sharing the wealth you mentioned."

The three laughed heartily, then continued on together, stopping first to get their breath and regain some semblance of composure. Now and then Inigo would break into a delighted chuckle, telling them again of his great fear.

Home! It had been a long time since Inigo had heard that word. It used to mean so much. But then, he had been a different person. The fire of the soldier of Loyola still burned in his heart, but now it warmed the bleak days of the sick, the poor and the unwanted aged, in one hospital after another. These were his family now; his home was with them. That indomitable flame was to light their dark days on earth and illumine the road to heaven.

It wasn't easy to convince the two servants that home was no longer the stately Loyola manor house. Despite his brother's invitation, Inigo was determined to lodge at the hospital in town, where he could be of real service. There he would be free to come and go, to take time teaching the children about God, to beg alms from house to house in penance and humility.

It wasn't long before the whole town was buzzing about the return of Inigo. Some who had known him as a boy reminisced about the past. "Remember Pamplona?" one old soldier recalled. "Inigo was brought home with a shattered leg. None of us thought he would pull through. He has a will of iron, that man! He recovered, but he was always different after that."

But the old timer didn't know *why* Ignatius had changed. As Inigo lay still day after day, with nothing but the sunlight on the wall to mark the passage of time, he had hit upon a way of making the hours of convalescence pass more quickly.

"Magdalena," he asked one morning, "could you bring me some books to while away the hours? Bring some good ones—romances—you know the kind I like."

Magdalena knew, all right. She smiled sweetly, as if to consent, then went about the house searching for just the right books. She loved Inigo as a son. When she had married Don Martin and come to live at Loyola, Inigo was still a child. Since his mother had died before he even knew her, Magdalena had become both sister and mother to the high-spirited youth. Now she saw her chance to make a lasting impression on the mind of Ignatius.

Inigo was propped up on pillows, staring blankly out the window.

"I've brought you a couple of books," announced Magdalena. "I think you'll like them."

"I knew I could count on you. What are they? New ones?" He took the two books and eagerly opened to the title page of one. As he read the title, he smiled good-naturedly at what he assumed was a joke. He read the title of the second and started to laugh.

"*The Life of Christ* and *The Lives of the Saints!* For sure, Magdalena, these *are* good books. But now, where are my romance stories?"

"I have brought you the two greatest romance stories that were ever written. Nothing can equal the love of Christ for us and the love of the saints for the Lord."

"Do you really mean it? Do you want me to read *these?*"

"They are the only books we have in the house. If you want to read, you will have to read these."

Thus ended the conversation. Magdalena left the room, and the smile left Inigo's face.

"Well," he mused, "if that's the way things stand, maybe if I finish these, she will be willing to get me some *real* romances."

He opened the *Life of Christ* and began to read. The present marched backward. Ignatius was in the hills of Galilee, walking with the Master. He stood with Him by the sea and heard the words of eternal life. He experienced the compassion of Christ and the thrill of the crowds over the healing of the blind and crippled. He indignantly approved when Christ ordered the money changers out of the temple; he experienced His mercy when He forgave the woman caught in adultery. He spent nights in prayer beside the Divine Master, and sensed His exhaustion after a day of preaching and healing.

Then time stood deathly still as he knelt beneath the cross to watch a crucified God die for him, a sinner. Horrified, he listened to the jeers and mockery of the throng. He felt the eyes of Christ pierce his soul as He uttered the words, "Father, forgive them; they do not know what they are doing." Beneath the cross stood Mary, Christ's mother, the only woman who was ever to claim the love of Ignatius of Loyola.

**"Lord,... you
have the words
of eternal life."**
John 6:68

The saints, Ignatius discovered, are the real soldiers of this world. All the fantastic adventures of chivalrous knights, all their deeds of love, all their sacrifices for earthly honors, faded into a colorless, lusterless background when he read about the adventures, love and sacrifices of the saints for God and their fellow men.

Where before had raged flames of passion, ambition, pride and vanity, now burned a steady, pure smokeless flame that was to set the world on fire for Christ. Had not Christ Himself said: "I have come to cast fire upon the earth"?

Magdalena watched the transformation of Inigo. She had hardly believed her eyes when she saw him avidly reading the books. He was so enthralled that he scarcely noticed her coming and going. Ignatius had found the King of kings. He pledged to do battle for Him without reserve, but his first battle was against himself. Once he had conquered himself, he was ready to conquer the world for Christ the King.

When Magdalena watched Inigo leave home, she must have known he would not long remain in the dress of a noble knight. He soon changed his clothes to those of a beggar; he changed his desires to those of the Lord. As a pilgrim, he wandered from place to place serving the sick whenever he could, begging for alms to be able to help the poor. His travel took him to the Holy Land, to the Jerusalem made holy by the Son of God made Man. His adventures were many, his sufferings greater than those any soldier was asked to bear.

Then, at thirty-three, he decided that the Lord wanted him to complete his education. He enrolled himself in an elementary school and attended classes with ten- and eleven-year-old boys, uniting himself with the Christ who was mocked as a laughing-stock.

Nothing could quench the flame that burned in that heart. Other men came within the circle of its heat and light and were equally fired by a tormenting love that only God could satisfy. This love gave them no rest. It set their feet moving in every direction to preach the Good News. It kept their hands busy helping the sick, the aged, the poor, the fallen dregs of humanity that hid in the dark places of every big city.

The number of Ignatius' followers grew.

"What are we to answer," one of the group questioned Ignatius, "if someone asks who we are? What shall we say?"

Until then, he had simply called their little group the "friends of Christ." By now their ideals had been fused and forged in the flame called Ignatius to become one great power idea.

"If anyone asks us who we are," he replied, "we shall answer we are of the Company of Jesus."

The newborn Company of Jesus spread out, like the spokes of a wheel, to speak of Christ to whomever would listen. It was then that Ignatius directed his steps toward the town of his childhood.

Is it any wonder if the rumors buzzed about *this* Ignatius, so different from the young man everyone remembered? Only Magdalena could stand back with the clear vision of the past and recognize the Inigo of the present. Perhaps she thought of what the outcome might have been had she provided the books he had requested. It is often said that a man *is* what he reads. Magdalena certainly took no convincing, for she beheld living proof.

The future was to be far more glorious. Battles were still to be fought by the new Society of Jesus, and the most important was the one for its very existence as a papally approved religious congregation. Victory was won, only the first of many — some spectacular, but most of them known to God alone.

Soon nation after nation, from the Orient to the Americas, was touched by the fire that filled many hearts with only one flame.

Like a candle that has consumed itself, so Ignatius found his strength failing more and more. He had served Christ his King generously, faithfully. He had loyal sons all over the world to carry forward the standard of Christ the King. He wasn't satisfied with his life; he could have done more, at least so he thought. But he was serene. He loved God and God loved him. That was enough. All for the greater glory of God.

Ignatius of Loyola died quietly, alone in his room. He had cherished his hours spent alone with God in the cave at Manresa. Perhaps God allowed him to spend his last hours on earth in intimate communion with his King, for that is all the reward St. Ignatius would have wanted. From that solitude he passed into the company of the angels and saints, where Christ Himself is the eternal reward.

9

set
the
world
on
fire!

It was November, 1552. A dejected figure stood on the shore, staring off into the distance. Only six miles away lay the Chinese mainland, its rugged coastline barely visible through the morning mist. Again, this morning, as on so many other mornings, Father Francis Xavier waited for the promised Chinese merchant junk—that again never came. His jaws set tight, Francis wrapped his paper-thin cloak around his shivering body and trudged back to his makeshift hut.

Sorely disappointed, he sank down onto his mat and buried his head in his hands. How lonely and frustrated he felt! It was quite clear that he would be unable to bring the Gospel of Christ into China.

All of a sudden, Francis felt a tide of anger welling up within him as he remembered the painful circumstances that had brought him to the lonely island of Sancian. "That meddlesome man, the governor," he muttered to himself. "It's all his fault that I'm here...." He felt again the terrible pain in his head from the sharp stone thrown at him. He heard once more the jeers of the crowd of demonstrators in Malacca. But then, before his old pride could get the upper hand, Francis reacted. "Father, forgive them," he mumbled half aloud. "Forgive them. It is *Your* will that I'm here. Forgive me, dear Lord, for my lack of confidence and love. Forgive me for my weakness." Yes, it was true that the governor of Malacca had upset all of Francis' plans and had given him personal offense. But what of it? It was God's will, and God would straighten things out in His own good time.

Pulling himself over to the low table, Francis penned his last letter. The cold November winds ripped the priest's wasted body as fever raced through him and his strength continued to seep away. "It's a long time," he wrote with a shaking hand, "since I felt so little inclined to go on living." He gave advice and counsel to the missionaries he had left behind in India, Malacca and Japan. As he wrote, the faces of all his friends and converts passed before him. Tears welled up in his eyes as he recalled their affection for him, their loyalty to the Gospel and to the person of Christ. How good they were! How unworthy he felt. Slowly and painfully, Francis folded the letter. He walked to his mat and fell on it. For some reason sleep wouldn't come.... Perhaps it was the bitter cold, or the fever, or perhaps...he felt that his end was near and he should review his life. So much had happened to him in forty-six years.

Real living had begun for Francis in 1534, when he had had to surrender to a little lame soldier-beggar, Ignatius of Loyola. Ignatius had constantly pounded him with the question, "What does it profit a man to gain the whole world but lose his soul?" Now Francis mused, "My, how I fought Ignatius, and how I fought

God, who was using Ignatius to call me to Himself. Didn't Ignatius tell me that I was the toughest dough he ever had to knead? My God, thank You for the grace to have been able to surrender to You and to the guidance and advice of my father in Christ, to embrace a life of poverty, humility, and obedience. Where would I be now if Ignatius had given up on me?" Beads of perspiration rolled down Francis' face as he remembered the wayward deeds of his youth.

Quiet calm returned to Xavier as he recalled his ordination day. How anxious and impatient he had been to start working for Christ! Only through much prayer, sacrifice and self-discipline had he been able to dominate his vain and pleasure-loving spirit, his impetuosity. By dint of sheer will power and generous response to God's grace, he had learned to wait patiently on the will of God.

And by means of his own experience, he became able to advise his comrades, "Each one should strive to win the battle of his own heart before setting out to reform others. The way to conquer fear is to find courage totally in God. The road of true progress for a man is to show himself great in little things."

As his fever rose higher and higher, Francis tossed and turned on his bed of pain. This fever reminded him of his power idea, the command Ignatius had given him when he had assigned him to the mission in India and the Orient: "Go and set the world on fire!" Yes, his body was being consumed with fever, but his life had already been consumed by the fire of the love of God and men that burned unceasingly in his heart. God had given him so much love that at times in his life he had had to tell Christ, "Enough, O Lord, enough! My heart cannot stand all the love You are giving me. Do not take these crosses away from me unless You give me heavier ones."

Eleven years before he lay dying on Sancian, Xavier had embarked on a staggering adventure for Christ. The sufferings of the thirteen-month voyage to India had tempered the steel in him and enlarged his heart. Once ashore, he had spent and overspent himself to bring the Gospel to those who knew it but didn't live it and to those who had never heard of it before. His mornings had been a ceaseless round of visits to the sick and imprisoned; his afternoons, a series of intensive catechism classes; his evenings, a round of Bible storytelling; his nights, a preparation of prayer and penance for the apostolate of the following day.

Xavier hadn't mastered all the Indian dialects right away, so he had simply acted as a Christian should. He knew how to smile, and smile he did! He had been firm when necessary. But rather than drive men away by pouring vinegar on their spiritual wounds, he had striven to draw them to Christ with the honey of compassion, understanding and kindness.

It had taken a great deal of courage to walk through the crowded streets, ringing his little bell and preaching in halting, imperfect speech. But he had had charts made to convey the Christian truths, and had set these same truths to catchy tunes and melodies that made them wing their way from village to village and port to port.

After three short years in India, Francis had been able to count 20,000 new Christians in thirty different villages. Then he had moved on to the Moluccas and Spice Islands, to continue "setting the world on fire." He couldn't rest as long as there was only one person in the world who didn't know Christ and the Christian message! Despite the tropical heat, despite three shipwrecks and constant danger from pirates and cannibals, he had labored for two years in that seething maze of islands and could number one hundred converts there.

Back to India, then, and off to Japan! Japan had never before met Christ. Many were the hardships, disappointments and successes. These successes, however, had been won at the cost of great personal sacrifice. But after two years in Japan, the fruits of Francis' mission had been consoling — over 2,000 converts.

It had all passed, now. As the hours slowly ebbed by, in the little hut on the island of Sancian, Francis' fever turned into delirium. He babbled incoherently. In his lucid moments, he would gaze out his door at the Chinese coast and heave deep sighs. "Oh, if only I could enter China! But it is not Your will, Lord. Your will be done. How many souls there are to reach yet! How many do not become Christians simply because they have no one to preach to them! Sometimes I wish I could run into some of the universities back in Europe and cry out like a madman to the people who are educated but do not use their learning to do good. If only they realized how many souls lose heaven because *they* sit by and do nothing about helping. Along with their other subjects they should study about their duty of using their God-given talents for You, O Lord. If only more people would realize what they can do to make this world a better place, to make people know You, Lord, and love You, and live for You, some day to be with You forever!"

As Francis lay dying, his faithful companion, Paul, a young Chinese Christian, kept his sorrowful vigil. He would one day give a detailed account of the last days of his dear father in Christ. But now he tried to shelter Francis from the piercing winds as best he could and knelt close to him so as not to miss a word.

Between his spells of delirium, Francis prayed continually, gazing at his beloved crucifix and murmuring, "Jesus, Son of David, have mercy on me. Mother of God, remember me!" Humanly speaking, it was a strange and sad end to his heroic labors for Christ. But what did that matter? "In You, O Lord, have I hoped!" he exclaimed. "Let me never be confounded!" "Jesus," he murmured softly.

It was December 3, 1552. Francis Xavier went to possess the Christ he had loved so much on earth. He had been a torch lifted high to dispel the darkness of error and sin. From that happy day in 1534, when he had said "Yes" to God, this man of fire had striven to conquer himself. It was because of this that God had blessed his labors and used him to bring the light of truth to thousands who otherwise would have remained in darkness.

10

nothing
by
halves

Calle Mayor was alive with activity. The wide street was thronged with excited clusters of curious townspeople, all eager for a look at the newest member of the emperor's court. The soft May sunshine of that day in 1528 gave everything in Alcalá de Henares a regal sort of glow.

A hush ran through the milling crowd. Bridles and spurs jingled in the distance, and scarlet livery flashed at the bend in the street. A long train of servants, their pack horses and mules in line, came slowly into view, followed by a young man riding erect on his prancing thoroughbred black. Young Borgia, not yet nineteen, smiled and nodded in acknowledgment of the many greetings. Anticipation flowed through his veins like wine. Cousin to Charles V, Francis looked forward to an active and successful career as one of the emperor's courtiers.

The grand pageant continued slowly down the Calle Mayor. Faces filled the balconies as well as the street. Unexpectedly the black was halted. A slight scuffle on the edge of the crowd had caught

Francis' attention, as four or five inquisitors in their black and white habits matter-of-factly hustled a new prisoner into custody.

In itself this certainly was not a scene to detain a young noble.

The prisoner, however, *did* look a bit unusual in his rough, sackcloth garment, gathered at the waist by a length of hemp. His bare feet and tousled beard gave him an odd sort of John-the-Baptist look. But other than that, it was common enough to see a university student being taken in for questioning....

However, he is older than most, thought Francis, probably in his thirties. And those eyes...! The young rider could hardly tear his gaze away from those piercing black eyes. What was there about this man that made him so different?

For a moment, Borgia forgot his courtly plans and dreams. In that one frozen second, he had a feeling of being known to his very depths. But then the crowd shifted, breaking the "spell." The clamor of the street pushed in on his consciousness again. Francis flicked the reins of his mount. He was smiling and waving once more, but in a small corner of his mind the face and eyes of that man had been forever engraved.

Later he learned the man's name—Ignatius of Loyola—but little did he realize what a part this ragged prisoner was to play in his life. Indeed, almost twenty years were to pass before Francis would see Ignatius again.

Francis was welcomed by the emperor more as a family member than as a subject. The young man's loyalty and real affection for his cousin deepened daily.

A year or more passed quickly in the company of Charles V and Empress Isabella. Borgia witnessed unforgettable pageantry and excitement in the visit of Fernando Cortez—the conquistador from the New World—who brought his monarch exotic gifts plundered from the Aztecs. He also learned of the thousand worries and cares that burdened the young emperor, and he did his best to help where he could.

In his frequent dealings with Charles and Isabella, Francis could not help but grow to know the empress' favorite ladies-in-waiting, Eleonor and Juana de Castro. The two sisters were of noble Portuguese birth, and had grown up with Isabella in Lisbon. Eleonor, especially, was inseparable from the queen. Her concern for her mistress was evident to all, and particularly to Francis. Although she was quiet and not extraordinarily beautiful, he saw in her the woman with whom he wanted to share his life.

The day came when he asked the queen for Eleonor's hand.

Isabella was delighted. Happiness sparkled in her eyes as she hurried off to ask the emperor.

She found her husband engrossed in papers and diplomatic "chess games" in his study. At the rustle of her gown, he looked up and smiled.

"Charles, listen," she breathed excitedly. "I think it's time for Eleonor to marry, don't you?"

"Hm-m-m. I imagine so," he answered slowly. He glanced back at his papers again. "Choose anyone you think would make her a suitable husband."

"Francis Borgia is a very upright young man and capable, too..." she ventured.

"I agree with you there," Charles replied, "but if you think for one minute that his father, the duke, would allow his heir to marry a 'foreigner'—well, you don't know the duke!"

But Isabella was quietly determined, and finally, to please her, the emperor signed a letter to the Duke of Gandia. A curt, barely polite refusal was not long in coming.

Francis would not be outdone, however, and one morning he suggested a plan to Charles as the two young men walked and talked together.

"There is just one thing that frightens my father," Francis began. "He simply cannot take the idea of leaving Gandia, even temporarily. He would agree to almost anything rather than do that."

Charles eyed his cousin quizzically. "So what do you have in that ever active mind of yours?"

"Well," Francis replied, "if he were to receive an invitation to come *here,* to court, to discuss the marriage...."

Charles chuckled and clapped Francis' shoulder. "You'll be a master diplomat someday!" he exclaimed.

July of 1529 saw the marriage of Eleonor de Castro and Francis Borgia in the imperial cathedral.

Each day of the seventeen years that followed brought them closer to one another and to their God. The first ten years were happy ones spent in the service of the emperor and empress. Charles, whose Hapsburg lands extended far beyond the confines of Spain, was often traveling to oversee the various sectors of his empire. So it was that Eleonor and Francis grew especially devoted to Isabella.

The eight Borgia children became accepted members of the imperial household as were their parents. Francis and Eleonor brought them up spiritually as well as materially. Husband and wife were of one mind and one soul in almost everything, and both felt that faith must be lived or else it quickly becomes a sham.

It was a rarity—that peace and happiness of theirs—but it was no accident. Daily "give-and-take" in all the hundreds of ordinary situations and aggravations accounted for the young couple's harmony. Francis and Eleonor strove to make the selflessness which is part of every parent's calling a habit in their dealings with each other, their children and their rulers.

Another spring cast a pale green shadow on the Castilian hills. It was the eleventh since the day Francis had arrived at court. The empress was in Toledo with her husband, the court, and, of course, the Borgias. All was light, airy and beautiful—until one morning Isabella did not come to breakfast.

Francis' fears were confirmed when his wife rushed up to him as he readied himself for the day's affairs.

"It's the fever again, Francis." She spoke through tight lips in a voice that quivered in its effort to keep from cracking.

"It's the same as when we were at Barcelona... only now she's not as strong...." Her voice trailed off into muffled sobs. Francis put his arm around Eleonor's shoulders. "We will pray"—he said huskily —"pray that God will spare her."

The days trickled slowly by. The best physicians were brought in; penance, prayer and Masses stormed heaven ceaselessly. But as April crawled to a close Isabella grew weaker and paler.

May 1, 1539, dawned clear and bright, but it might as well have been midwinter in Toledo. Haggard and dark-eyed from lack of sleep, Eleonor stumbled out of the empress' room and into her husband's arms.

"She's gone."

The dry whisper was like a thunderclap to Francis. Husband and wife were silent. "My God, have mercy!" Francis choked out. There was nothing else to say.

Francis never felt quite the same about life and his part in it after that. The years that followed were filled with ever stricter self-discipline. Only his wife knew of the hair shirt he began wearing. He was raised to the rank of marquis and given the high office of Viceroy of Catalonia. As he struggled to administer justice in the face of almost insurmountable odds, he struggled equally hard in training his own fiery nature, and channeling it to God.

1543 found the Borgias in Gandia, Francis being its duke now that his father had died.

March of 1546 came, and with it Eleonor's final illness. Francis prayed as he never had before; surely God would restore her to him and his children. One day as he knelt before the crucifix in his private chapel, he was stunned by a voice saying, "Francis, if you wish to keep the duchess with you longer, you may. But it is not the best for you."

Francis trembled as he answered.

"Are You leaving such a choice in *my* hands, my Lord and God? I want only what You want, because who better than You knows what is best...? You have given me everything I have; I beg You, dispose of everything as You will!"

His surrender was accepted. Eleonor died a few days later.

Francis knew that he must leave Gandia. He felt drawn to that new Order in the Church which called itself the Company of Jesus. His only desire now was to give himself totally and irrevocably to God's service. As he wrote his first inquiry to Ignatius of Loyola in Rome, he must have thought back to their meeting so long before.

Having provided for his children, Francis left Gandia for the last time four years after Eleonor's death. He had already made vows privately under

Ignatius' guidance and in the presence of some of the Jesuits of the University of Gandia.

Once in Rome, and for the rest of his life, the one-time duke and marquis sought only to serve. He waited on tables, helped in the kitchen, and avoided every reference to his former position.

It was not easy. In spite of his work at self-domination before, he still felt quite keenly the demands that obedience and total donation made upon him.

Ordained in 1551, Father Francis spent his remaining twenty-one years in active, selfless service to Christ and His Church in whatever obedience required of him. For eight years he was Commissary General for Spain, Portugal and the Indies. He traveled constantly, opening new houses and spurring the members of the older ones to greater zeal in their life for God.

It was no wonder that, in 1561, this embarrassingly humble yet immensely capable man was recalled to Rome to serve as the Order's Vicar General.

Four years later, following the death of Lainez, the second Jesuit General, Francis' sorrows were multiplied. The day of his election as Superior General of the Company of Jesus he spoke of as "the day of my crucifixion." After an intense period of spiritual exercises, Francis begged his fellow Jesuits to treat him as a "beast of burden" in his new office.

Again he was on the move, either through his numerous letters to Jesuits in every part of the world, or in his journeys through Spain, Portugal, France and Italy. He gave every ounce of his strength to his God.

His final journey nearly ended in Lyons, where his fever-racked body collapsed in a heap one morning after Mass.

But Francis would not be deterred. "I must die in Rome..." he constantly insisted. "Hurry, hurry, for the love of God!"

More dead than alive, Francis was carried on a rough litter through France to the Italian border and Turin. Almost literally inching their way, the sorrowing brothers made slow progress south.

It was September when the dying General made the last of his many visits to the house of our Lady at Loretto, and continued on the painful last few miles to Rome.

Finally he was laid on his own rough bed in a tiny cell adjoining the chapel. Unthinking crowds of visitors forced themselves upon him until he had to beg them to go. "Leave me," he whispered, "for now I only have time for God."

A few of the priests closest to him were allowed to stay. At last he could be at peace and think of God alone. For hours on end he was lost in prayer.

"Is there anything you would like, Father Francis?" Brother Marcos asked that last night. "I want only Jesus," came the barely audible reply. Peaceful and serene, obedient to his last breath, Father Francis Borgia began "true life" a little after midnight on October 1, 1572.

He had given his entire self to every duty — from that of a father and husband to that of a religious and priest. As he had lived, so he died. Totality was his hallmark and the heritage he left.

11

Poland's
eagle

The afternoon of July 25, 1564, was hot and sultry as a black cloud settled over the city of Vienna and warned the inhabitants of an approaching summer downpour. The blue Danube turned gray and lazily slapped in little ripples against the large granite structures lining its embankments.

A few miles outside of the city three horsemen reined in at a wayside inn and dismounted. Two of them were very well dressed.

"Looks like we're in for some rain," boomed the third, with a Polish accent. The pounding of his heavy boots woke the innkeeper from his afternoon reverie.

With visions of the day's income dancing before his eyes, the welcoming host all but fell over himself in his effort to serve his guests.

"We'll be spending the night here and will go into the city tomorrow, so we'll need lodging and a good meal. What have you got in the line of drink? We've come a long way." Thus spoke short, well-fed, middle-aged John Bilinski, whose manner bordered on the vulgar. He tore off his feathered hat and flung it across a table, revealing a perfectly round and highly-polished bald head.

The innkeeper eyed the three curiously. The other two were young men—boys, to be more exact. Paul Kostka, as he later found out, was almost sixteen, and Stanislaus, his brother, fourteen. Both were tall, handsome and mannerly. But it could easily be seen that Paul had been completely taken in by Bilinski's rough ways and was trying his utmost to imitate him. The innkeeper wondered how two fine lads such as these could have been entrusted to a man like Bilinski; but he held his tongue in check.

Stanislaus was different from his two traveling companions. While they threw themselves onto the soft beds for a short nap, he busied himself downstairs. He set the table and helped the innkeeper prepare supper.

"It was a long journey from Poland to Vienna, wasn't it?" queried the innkeeper.

"Yes," Stanislaus said softly. "But, thanks be to God, it was a safe one. It must have been my good mother's prayers. I miss her a lot. But I have my brother and a tutor with me. We'll be attending classes at the Jesuit College. What's it like there?"

Ump, thought the innkeeper. If all the nobility and gentry were as kind and amiable as this lad, we'd have no more problems.

"Ah—er. What was that? I mean, yes, yes, the Jesuit College is a fine place. They're all good teachers and holy priests. I'm sure you'll enjoy it."

The next morning found the threesome riding toward the city at a leisurely pace. The storm hadn't cooled things one bit. Lush, green foliage barely stirred as the scorching sun quickly dried the early morning dew. Birds chirped merrily, and singing cicadas promised that it would get even hotter.

The rector of the Jesuit College warmly welcomed the two sons of the Polish noble, Count Kostka. He showed them around the grounds and college church and then directed them to a large boarding house on campus. These living quarters had been given to the Society by the Emperor Ferdinand, who had founded the college a few years earlier.

Everything went along smoothly for eight months.

Although the subjects were somewhat difficult, Stanislaus applied himself as best he could. He studied far into the night and frequently fell asleep with his texts and notebooks in his hands. His marks improved, thus giving him a bit more free time. Instead of losing himself in idleness or drifting, however, Stanislaus did advanced studying and spent more time in spiritual reading and prayer.

Paul was quite the opposite. He and his friends spent their time reeling around the city half drunk.

When Emperor Ferdinand died, his son, Maximilian, demanded that the Jesuits return the boarding house to him.

Things could not have turned worse for Stanislaus.

Bilinski found a lodging for them with a man of ill-repute. Stanislaus' life-style was a silent reproach, and his landlord grew to hate him bitterly as time passed. Paul and Bilinski also turned against the younger lad and threatened to beat him unless he changed his ways. In fact, when the threats were of no avail, they actually did beat him and made him undergo sufferings of other sorts. One day they went so far as to drag in a woman of the streets to tempt him. But just the sight of Stanislaus, whose goodness and purity were unquestionable, impelled the woman to flee from the house in remorse.

Not once did Stanislaus ever reveal to his parents, the count and countess, what he had to undergo. He went out of his way to be kind to Paul, but this only served to infuriate his older brother more. Paul's anger soon turned to downright hatred.

Although Stanislaus bore it bravely, the pain and sorrow proved to be too much for him. A week before the Christmas of his third year in Vienna, he fell very ill. The doctors could do nothing. Bilinski and Paul were terrified. Hadn't they been the cause of this sickness?

Stanislaus was aware of the gravity of his condition and asked to receive the last sacraments. "Go to the church," he begged. "Ask the Fathers to bring the Blessed Sacrament to me, so I may receive Communion before I die."

Kimberger, the owner of the house and a man directly opposed to religion, had already warned Bilinski: "Be sure of this, I will never allow a priest to step into my house." Therefore, Bilinski completely ignored Stanislaus' request. Paul followed suit.

It was useless. All Stanislaus could do, then, was have recourse to heaven.

Day after day he grew worse. Then, on Christmas Eve, he received a unique gift while merrymakers were going their way in the snowy world outside, completely unaware that a miracle was taking place.

The candle had just flickered out and Stanislaus lay quiet in his bed. Suddenly a soft light flooded the room, and the Mother of Jesus appeared, holding the divine Child in her arms. The boy was too weak to rise, but he held out his arms, and our Lady placed her Child in them. Immediately, new life pulsed through Stanislaus' weakened body and he felt perfectly healthy again. The Blessed Virgin told him it was God's will that he enter the Society of Jesus as soon as possible. After she had said this, the vision ended, and Stanislaus again found himself in the darkness. But now he was completely well.

When Bilinski came the next morning, Stanislaus jumped up. "Give me my clothes," he exclaimed. "We'll go to Mass together and thank God!" Bilinski thought the boy was delirious and forbade him to get out of bed. However, the doctors who were called in to examine him found him in excellent condition. Bilinski finally broke down and went to church with Stanislaus.

Paul knew that Stanislaus had wanted to become a Jesuit ever since his arrival in Vienna. Therefore, when his younger brother redoubled his prayers and devotions Paul began to feel uneasy.

Stanislaus knew that his brother would never allow him to pursue his ideal. In fact, neither would the Jesuit superiors. They were afraid of incurring the wrath of Count Kostka. Stanislaus was his favorite son, and they knew the count had very different plans for the youth.

But Stanislaus could not "keep God waiting," as he phrased it. Turning to one of the older and more experienced Jesuit priests, he confided that the desire to become a Jesuit was not only his own, but that of God's Mother as well.

The good priest saw something extraordinary in the lad and suggested that he request permission to enter the Society from the superior of Augsburg, Germany. This superior was none other than Peter Canisius, whose name was also to be prefixed with an "St." "If he refuses you," the priest went on, "ask the Superior General, Father Francis Borgia, in Rome."

"How far is Augsburg, Father?" asked Stanislaus.

"Only 300 miles," the old Jesuit replied.

Only 300 miles! Stanislaus began to wonder how he would make it. But he reached a decision quickly. No price was too high to pay for his vocation. "I'll go." And go he did.

A few days later, the youth slipped out of the house dressed in poor traveling clothes, and set out for Augsburg.

Paul and a search party went after him, but Stanislaus outwitted his pursuers. The band returned to Vienna somewhat dismayed, while Stanislaus finally fulfilled his one desire. Father Peter Canisius accepted him into the Society of Jesus.

Prudence, however, counseled Father Canisius to send the young postulant to Rome. There, the good priest felt, Stanislaus would be farther away from Poland, and his father would think twice before undertaking such a long journey in search of him.

On October 25, 1567, Stanislaus Kostka arrived in the Eternal City.

Meanwhile, back in Vienna, Paul and Bilinski made preparations for an immediate return to Rostkow, Poland. The sight of the family castle did anything but awaken joy in their hearts. Over and over they rehearsed the story they would tell the Count.

When they had finished their tale—of course omitting any mention of the cruel treatment Stanislaus had undergone—the father was thoroughly infuriated. "That boy is a disgrace to himself and to our family!" he thundered. "A Kostka crossing Europe like a tramp to beg for admission into the Jesuits? What madness! What a fool! I'll never let another Jesuit into Poland...." On and on he raged.

Stanislaus' mother, however, read between the lines. Long before this, when Stanislaus was still very young, she had had presentiments about his future greatness.

It was decided that Paul would go to Rome and force Stanislaus to return to Poland. Paul set off, traveling slowly and making frequent stops along the way. All the fuss and inconvenience had only revived his hatred for Stanislaus. In fact, he did not arrive in Rome until over a year after Stanislaus' flight from Vienna.

He found suitable lodgings for himself and his attendants and then went immediately to visit a friend of his father's. As he told the dumfounded gentleman how Stanislaus had run away from Vienna and disgraced the Kostka name, his fury blazed up again. The gentleman looked at Paul with astonishment and then stammered, "I can assure Your Excellency that no Jesuit will hinder your brother's return home. I'm sure that if you go at once to their house at Santa Andrea you will be fully satisfied."

As Paul dashed out the door, one of his attendants ran up to him breathlessly:

"Have you heard? Have you heard?"

"Heard what?"

"Stanislaus is dead. He died a month ago. All Rome is calling him the Polish saint."

It was a different Paul who fell on his knees and wept like a child at Stanislaus' tomb next to the high altar of the Jesuit church.

Then, still sobbing, Paul heard the details of his brother's death from the lips of the superior.

Stanislaus had spent only ten months in Rome, but his memory would not easily be erased. He had done nothing great or outstanding. He had simply loved God with every fiber of his being and observed the Jesuit rule to perfection.

He had predicted the date of his own death, which had occurred on August 15, the feast of the Assumption of our Lady.

Stanislaus was only eighteen. He had been in Rome but a short time, yet crowds flocked to his funeral and people prayed continually at his tomb.

Thus, Stanislaus Kostka, "being made perfect in a short time," proved to be a real glory to his family name.

He had won for himself the promises of the beatitudes:

"Blest too the peacemakers; they shall be called sons of God.

Blest are those persecuted for holiness' sake; the reign of God is theirs.

Blest are you when they insult you and persecute you and utter every kind of slander against you because of me.

Be glad and rejoice, for your reward is great in heaven..." (Mt. 5:9-12).

12

an
intrepid
soldier

Our story opens in the large mission church on the Island of Santo Domingo, in the year 1509. Seventeen years before, Columbus had discovered this island. Now it suffered the throes of Spanish conquest. The conquistadors came to Santo Domingo, and to the rest of Latin America, seeking fame, wealth and glory at the cost of their own lives — and the lives of peoples they captured.

It was Sunday morning. Father Montesinos walked to the main altar with a slow, deliberate step. Genuflecting reverently, he silently pleaded, "Lord, strengthen me in proclaiming Your word." He turned and climbed the steps to the pulpit. Standing erect and silent, Father Montesinos glared at the faces before him. His congregation consisted of men hardened by war, risk-taking, suffering, brutality, greed, ambition and intrigue. To the right, in his special stall, the governor and his aids sat stiffly in their elaborate silks and satins and ruffled, starched collars, trying their best to look pious. To the left, metal-helmeted soldiers stood or sat at attention, their rugged features set off by their gleaming armor, and their cautious hands resting on their swords and daggers.

"Gentlemen," the preacher began, "you who profess yourselves to be Christians are making a mockery out of our holy Faith and are disgracing the royal crown with your evil deeds!" He stopped to let the words sink in. He didn't have long to wait. Angry stares and puffed, red faces warned him not to go on if he knew what was good for him. But go on he must. "You must stop the atrocities you commit against the Indians, God's poor children!" The priest knew he was lighting a powder keg, and the explosion came fast. Unmindful of where they were, the men raised clenched fists and angry voices in a tumult of shouts and threats, "You pious good-for-nothing, you have no right to tell us how to govern this province or how to be soldiers. Stick to your prudish praying!"

Father Montesinos shouted out over the din, continuing his public denunciation of their crimes, listing them one by one. Some of the more furious scrambled over others in an attempt to reach the preacher and silence him once and for all. Others with cooler heads shoved them back. "You call yourselves Christians," thundered Father Montesinos, "but do you *act* like Christians?"

The stinging question silenced one of the soldiers. Stunned, he stopped still like a blind man who suddenly saw the light. His soul-searching brought forth a painful answer: "No, I have not acted as a Christian." Bartholomew de las Casas hung his head in shame. Standing rooted in his place, he did not notice the governor unceremoniously puff his way out of the church or the soldiers swarm for the exit, darting searing glances at the preacher. He was thinking.

Bartholomew's father had shipped with Christopher Columbus back in 1492. He himself had sailed on the third voyage in 1498. For eleven years his only ideal had been adventure, the capture of new lands, and personal gain, at any cost. Now, at the age of thirty-five, he had suddenly come to the realization of what it meant to *really be a Christian*. Never before had he even bothered to ask himself whether the Lord approved of the slaughter and enslavement of the Indians of the New World.

Hideous scenes of massacres, tortures, and forced labor pierced his conscience. In a matter of only twenty years, the conquistadors had been responsible for the deaths of thousands upon thousands of natives — all of them perpetrated in the name of Christ and the Spanish Crown! He, as a conquistador, felt himself an accomplice to all this slaughter. He must make amends, somehow. As a promising young officer with a very bright career ahead of him, and prospects of abundant wealth, Bartholomew decided.

Setting his own slaves free, Bartholomew sold his villa and possessions and sought instruction at the Dominican monastery. His faith, eagerness and utterly sincere intention deeply moved the superior. The former conquistador closed the door behind him and entered upon a whole new life. Due to the fact of the scarcity of priests and missionaries, Bartholomew's training was hurried, but it was profound.

In less than two years, he became Father Bartholomew de las Casas. The conqueror had been conquered; the intrepid soldier of the king had become the fearless champion of the Indians.

Almost immediately, the new priest launched an all-out campaign for the rights of the oppressed natives. Resolute, he withstood his own countrymen to the face, unmasked their hypocrisy, and denounced their depravity from the pulpit.

The great landowners and powerful slave traders hated him. Who did this young upstart think he was, anyway? With all his fine words and utopian ideas, he would be the destruction of the Spanish kingdom in the New World! Why, if he kept up this insane meddling, he would ruin all commerce and industry! Bartholomew was like a thorn in their side.

With a soldier's determination, Bartholomew tramped up and down craggy mountains, dangled from vines as he swayed over bottomless ravines, pushed through steaming jungles, maneuvered flimsy boats through swollen rivers and struggled against merciless tropical diseases. He would stop at nothing to bring the *real* Gospel message to his beloved Indian brothers. For the next thirty-five years, neither man nor beast deterred him from following his purpose. He went everywhere. Almost every corner of the New World knew this kindly man, this Christian who was different from the rest. Whole villages would turn out to meet him and be converted at his preaching. One month he was in Peru, the next in Guatemala, the next in Santo Domingo, and another in Mexico. To the downtrodden natives, he was, in their own words, "Father to the Indians."

Although his countrymen still hated him with a passion, they were forced to recognize his obvious holiness.

At one point, thousands of conscripted laborers were brought into Santo Domingo. They were later refused permission to return to their native lands. All the natives in the city rose up in rebellion and killed two Dominican missionaries. Retaliation was speedy. The governor ordered the massacre and complete destruction of not only the Indian village in question, but every Indian village in the entire province!

"You beast," roared Bartholomew. The table cracked under his fist. "You can't do that! You're only the governor acting in the name of the king. Great as the crime is, it doesn't warrant a mass killing in the province. The King of Spain would never command such a thing! In God's name, revoke your order!"

"And you, you...stay out of the affairs of the kingdom, you cowardly, soft-peddling preacher!" shouted the enraged governor. "How do we know that you yourself weren't involved in the killing? You put the Indians up to it, turning them against lawful authority!"

"Now wait a minute, Your Excellency. Never once have I told the natives to rebel. If they have, it's because your oppression is beyond human endurance. And if I'm yelling, it's because you're so deaf!"

A mob quickly formed outside the governor's palace. Abuse upon abuse was heaped upon Bartholomew and he had to flee for his life while the order for the carnage was ruthlessly carried out. The "Father of the Indians" could only weep for his poor children.

The valiant missionary kept right on with his fight for the rights of the Incas and Aztecs. If the authorities in the New World would not listen, he would appeal to the King himself. He wrote letters. He crossed the Atlantic no less than five times to appeal for justice and charity. Charles V listened attentively to de las Casas and the "simple, humble, patient and faithful" Indians he brought as eyewitnesses. The King listened to the conquistadors, "furious wolves, tigers and hungry lions" who seemed demented in their passion for killing.

In a book called *The Destruction of the Indians*, Father Bartholomew wrote a point-by-point account of the inhumanity practiced in the New World.

The book proved a sensation in Spain. People were aghast at the cruelties practiced against other human beings. Public opinion was so strong that the King made new laws, abolished slavery, and appointed new leaders. He sent these trusted men to the New World to put the revised laws into effect.

But despite the changes, the overall situation remained as bad as before. The aging Father de las Casas was appointed a bishop. At his request, he was sent to a poor, undeveloped region.

For ten more years, Bishop Bartholomew continued his efforts to alleviate the sufferings inflicted on the helpless. Then, at the age of eighty, he again sailed for Spain to champion the Indians' cause. But the New World was a long way from the mother country, and as often happens, the wicked frustrated the good will of their ruler. Too many conquistadors had too many friends and relatives at court and in the noble ranks. Too many Spaniards had commercial and mining interests in the lands across the sea. Gold blinded their hearts and made them hard. One day tragic news reached the ears of de las Casas —thousands of Indians had been killed in an uprising in Peru. The sorrow was too much for him to bear and he suffered a stroke. And yet, the aged prelate would not give up. Unable to sail again for the New World because of partial paralysis, he wrote in defense of his children from a monastery where he had taken up residence. He wrote and wrote until he died broken and sorrowful at the age of ninety-two.

The plight of the oppressed in the New World would end only after more than twenty million Indians had died. But because of Bartholomew de las Casas the Indians knew that not all men are evil. They knew that God loved them, as did de las Casas and many others who would spend their lives giving dedicated testimony to the principles of the Gospel.

13

just
Father
Michael

It was January 7, 1566. A chill lay in the air, but the bright sun promised a warmer day. Even though it was still early, St. Peter's Square had already become a milling sea of faces. All eyes were focused in anticipation on a lone workman. Brick by brick, he unsealed one of the walled-up windows of the conclave. Nearly a month had gone by since Pope Pius IV had passed away, and all Rome, in fact the entire Catholic world, was waiting for the cardinals to elect a new Pontiff. This morning the signal had come: a decision had been reached!

An excited hush settled on the square as the familiar figure of a young cardinal, Charles Borromeo, appeared in the now-open window.

"We have a new Pope," he declared solemnly: "Pius V!"

As Borromeo stepped back into the room, the crowd outside broke into unrestrained cheers. The cry "Viva il Papa!" rang on every side.

113

Borromeo watched the slight, straight figure of the sixty-two-year-old Dominican, Cardinal Alexandrian, as he made his way to the window to greet the crowds for the first time as Christ's Vicar. Charles felt sure that the Holy Spirit would be able to work quite well through this new Shepherd; the Council of Trent had just been completed, and a man of convictions and will power was needed to carry its reforms into reality.

The Pontiff himself was full of his own thoughts. As he gazed over the immense throng, the responsibility of his office settled more firmly on his shoulders, and a stab of momentary fear ran through his frame. I can't do it by myself! his soul cried out. But just as quickly he answered himself, Michael, you are not alone....

"Michael," the Pope smiled to himself. How many simple joys that name called up in his memory! How he wished he could have remained always "just Father Michael...."

But Michael Ghislieri had never been "just" anything. Every step of his life he had poured all he had into being and doing the best he could at each moment.

The Pope thought back on how his life for Christ had begun....

That day was a sweltering one in the meadow just outside Bosco. Anthony (his baptismal name) leaned gratefully against the trunk of a gnarled, old shade tree and mopped his face. The sheep grazed peacefully, leaving him free to think. Life was just beginning at fourteen, and there was so much he wanted to be and *do!*

"Dad would like me to learn some trade," he thought out loud, "which is fine with me. I only wish there were some way I could study more — I know I'm lucky to have received the schooling I did, since it's so expensive...but there must be so much more one could learn — especially about God...." His voice trailed off thoughtfully as he caught sight of two distant figures on the road. They shimmered and danced in the heat, but as they came closer, Anthony's squinting eyes could make out the black and white habits of Dominican friars. His heart leaped, as the hopes, desires and prayers of the past months suddenly congealed into one firm conviction: Perhaps this was the answer — he would be a Dominican!

Eagerly Anthony jogged across the meadow and intercepted the friars. But suddenly he did not know what to say. It took him a moment to untie his embarrassment-knotted tongue and greet the priests.

"Do you live around here, son?" they inquired, smiling at his excitement and obvious pleasure.

"Yes, Father, just down the road a bit," Anthony answered, still panting a little. Then the whole story let loose. Like an avalanche, his words tumbled over each other as he told of waiting, wondering, and praying; of his desire to know his God and his Faith more deeply. "Father, do you think I could become a Dominican brother?" he concluded.

The two men glanced at each other. The way this boy spoke showed both sincerity and maturity. "We're on our way back to our monastery in Voghera, now," they said. "If your parents are willing, you can come with us."

In his new life, Anthony Ghislieri, the Dominican novice, gave his all, just as he always had in everything from trimming grapevines and tending sheep to carrying out his earliest studies. Every problem was faced squarely for the Lord and for His Church. The years just couldn't seem to wait for each other to pass;

soon the novice had taken his religious vows and was preparing for ordination.

The glorious day came, and Anthony Ghislieri became Father Michael — forever. Just Father Michael, always, he thought. His only desire was simply to live the Dominican way of life in its total and original purity until the day he died.

But goodness and talent have a way of being noticed, no matter how diligently they are hidden; shortly after his ordination Father Michael was made a lector in theology and philosophy. For sixteen years he taught these subjects and strove, at the same time, to deepen his knowledge of the mind of his founder. "There's one thing about Father Michael," more than one friar was heard to remark: "He is a *Dominican* to the core. To talk with him about Father Dominic, you would think he had met him in person."

For a considerable time, Father Michael was also novice master and had a share in the cares of governing his Order. Ghislieri accepted each new duty, each new anxiety, as God's will for him. "I certainly would not have chosen these myself," he once affirmed half-laughingly.

In 1542, Pope Paul III revived the Roman Inquisition in an effort to restore the fullness of the Faith to his flock. As the Dominicans had been placed in charge of this task, Father Michael's superiors searched for men whose knowledge of the Faith and whose own religious observance equipped them for the office. It was not surprising that Michael of Alexandria (as he was called, after the large city nearest his home village) was soon assigned to Como as an inquisitor. There he dealt with stiff opposition from merchants who insisted on diffusing books filled with spiritual poison to the townspeople. With greater ease, he also visited and instructed as many families as possible, both there in the city and also in the numerous tiny hamlets nestled in the hills. He found that, in most cases, mistaken ideas were due only to lack of education and awareness of the beauty the Church's doctrines contained. Being kind, understanding and extremely clear in his explanations, he was able to win many of the faithful to full communion.

Still continuing his inquisition duties, Father Michael was made bishop of two small dioceses in 1556. Only a year later, an assignment as commissary general of the Inquisition and elevation to the cardinalate were added to his burden.

When one well-meaning person tried to congratulate him on all these "honors," Ghislieri ruefully answered, "They are like so many iron chains riveted about my feet to prevent my slipping off to the quiet of the cloister ever again. But," he added, smiling, "I believe they are all bricks in God's great design, so we must simply do our utmost to build with them in the best way possible, no matter how heavy they are! God will provide the mortar and the strength."

His new duty as commissary general gave him the opportunity of visiting the prison daily and speaking with the men. His approach was a fine blend of kindness and common sense, which helped many to reconsider their position and repent.

One such man was Sixtus of Siena. The young Franciscan had been a popular preacher until he began spreading false ideas which he had learned before becoming a religious. He thought he was right, and no one had yet been able to convince him otherwise.

The friar's misery was obvious, and when Ghislieri passed by, he was quick to notice. "What's your name, son?" the Dominican began. The whole story was not long in coming, once Sixtus realized the sincerity of this man of God.

"I will come to see you again," the commissary general promised as he left that first day. "In the meantime, pray."

Alexandrian, as Ghislieri was also called, took his own advice and began storming heaven for the young friar. His Masses and Communions, his rosaries and other prayers were all offered for one purpose — Sixtus of Siena.

On a morning not long after, Alexandrian again visited the young friar's cell. "You are still fighting aren't you, Sixtus?" he remarked.

"What good is it, even if I do live?" the young man replied. "I could never go back to my Order — I've disgraced it too much! It's much better to die — there is nothing else!"

"That's the easy way, my son," Ghislieri chided gently. "Wouldn't it be harder to live a life of penance than to die?"

Suddenly the younger man burst into tears. "For that," he managed to say huskily, "I might be willing to live!"

Sixtus was pardoned, received absolution from Alexandrian himself and was quietly admitted to the Dominican Order. As he went on to become one of the greatest Scripture scholars of his century, Sixtus never forgot the commissary general and what he had done. "To that man," he once declared, "I owe not only my temporal welfare, but also my eternal salvation!"

Then came that fateful day in the month-old conclave following the death of Pius IV.

Cardinal Alexandrian, or "just Father Michael," as far as he himself was concerned, had been kneeling in his room, a simple religious in touch with his God. Steps sounded in the hall and a determined knock jarred the door. What a wave of disbelief ran through him! How he trembled as he murmured his acceptance.

And now, here he was, giving the blessing of the Holy Father to the cheering crowds. A new life lay ahead. Pius V turned back into the room and called Cardinal Borromeo to his side.

"Charles," he began, "we have some things to take care of before the coronation. I want you to do a bit of investigating—make a list of the hospitals and the poorest families here in Rome, the very poorest. Instead of the usual shower of coins in the square at the time of the coronation, twice the normal amount is to be distributed privately to these families. Then also," the Pope looked up with a sparkle of joy in his eyes, "instead of providing a banquet for the cardinals, the ambassadors and dignitaries, we will send these funds to the poorer convents throughout the city. Not one is to be skipped, mind you!"

"Your Holiness," Borromeo smiled, "this will cause quite a stir, I'm sure you know!"

"And so will *all* of Trent's decisions, Borromeo. We are going to live by the Council and bring its hopes into reality. The Bride of Christ deserves to be restored to her full beauty."

The six short years of Pius V's reign were marked by intense activity and deep prayer. His own personal holiness so profoundly impressed those who met him, that—in many instances—they began to imitate him spontaneously. The reforms were numerous and carried out in a spirit of fatherly determination, in spite of increasing illness.

The Pope was strictest of all with himself. "Your Holiness," a young bishop once ventured to admonish, "you shouldn't fast so much. True, it is Lent, but you are not well, and surely it is not expected...."

The Pope smiled weakly, realizing that he must have let his pain show in his expression and bearing. Lately the spasms had been doubling him up at night in agony. He made a quiet resolution to conceal his suffering more carefully. But the fast-advancing disease would soon make that impossible.

"My son," he replied to the bishop, "if we do not have some little sacrifices to offer the Lord, what *do* we have? And there are so many things to pray for...."

He was thinking now of the coming sea battle with the Turks. The Christian world had to be freed from the constant threat of invasion, and somehow he felt that this approaching event would be decisive. There had to be prayer, much prayer. All the city was urged to beg heaven's Queen to obtain success.

It is a fact of history that the battle of Lepanto turned out to be a total Christian victory.

The very afternoon on which the struggle occurred found Pius V in the papal study with a few of the cardinals. Suddenly he turned abruptly and walked to the window. He opened it and stood staring out for quite some time, his eyes fixed on the sky.

The cardinals looked at one another wonderingly. At last, closing the window after him, the Pope turned and said quietly, "This is no time to talk of business! Let us thank Almighty God that our forces have gained a great victory over the Turks!" Amazement was clearly written on every face. Two weeks later, messengers from the fleet arrived to confirm the Pope's words. All Rome knew it was God who had fought for them, and the entire city joined in fervent thanksgiving. In memory of the great event, Pius V had the invocation to Mary, Help of Christians, inserted into the litany of our Lady, and he instituted the feast of the Holy Rosary, to be celebrated on October 7, the anniversary of the victory.

Only three months after the tremendous battle and victory at Lepanto, for which he had worked and prayed so intensely, Pius V's ever-present illness made itself felt with alarming intensity. He himself believed that this was to be the end, even though his friends hoped he could revive. Toward the latter part of April, the Pope announced decisively, "I have no more business to take care of except my business with God. The account of all the deeds and words of my life which I shall soon have to give to Him requires that I use all my powers to prepare for it."

May 1, 1572, was nearly spent. A brilliant sunset caused a Spanish Carmelite nun of Avila to pause on her way to chapel and give silent praise to the Almighty. Suddenly she stood riveted to the spot. An elderly man in the white habit of a Dominican stood before her. Teresa of Avila stared as she recognized Pope Pius V.

"Teresa," he said, "the work you are doing for the Church and your Order will never be forgotten. I promise to help you...from heaven." With that he was gone.

Teresa entered the chapel and faced her nuns assembled in the choir. "Do not be surprised to see me weeping," she said haltingly. "You, too, should weep with me—for today the Church has lost her greatest shepherd."

14

human
and
holy

It was a warm, sunny day in the early summer of 1530. The spacious sixteenth-century home of Don Alphonso de Cepeda rocked with the laughter and merriment of his eleven children, eight nieces and nephews and countless in-laws and friends. Maria de Cepeda, Don Alphonso's oldest daughter, had just been married. Music, song and dance made everyone tingle with emotion. Gleeful little ones, always ready for a party, scampered up and down corridors, darting in and out of ballrooms and dining halls, while elegantly dressed lords and ladies speculated on love, politics and fortunes, and blushing couples swirled to the rhythmic swells of lutes, harps, and harpsichords.

Don Alphonso surveyed the grand scene, and his lips parted in a faint smile. It had been very hard to smile this past year and a half since he had lost his charming wife, Beatrice. She had been so good, so beautiful, so efficient and so youthful....

A burst of laughter freed Don Alphonso from his sad thoughts. Beatrice lived on in her children!

123

At that moment a twitter of excitement rushed through the room. One of Don Alphonso's daughters had just entered. Teresa's jet-black hair fell to her shoulders in soft curls, accenting her fair complexion and flushed cheeks. Her luminous eyes danced with laughter and lit up her full, oval face. Her graceful figure was complemented by a modest gown, bright orange in color, bordered with black velvet bands. With all the grace of her fifteen years, she glided across the floor, curtsied and kissed her father's hand. A group her own age then rushed her off to a corner of the ballroom to enjoy her wit and bubbling personality. Though also gentle and gracious, the young girl thrilled everyone with her vivacity, warmth, and generous efforts to please.

Don Alphonso watched Teresa for a few moments. His eyes suddenly narrowed and his face clouded when another young woman joined Teresa's group. As a relative, this cousin had frequent access to the de Cepeda household.

Lightheaded, fond of novels and extremely vain, this silly girl was exerting a bad influence on his fifteen-year-old daughter. Teresa had changed greatly. She, too, was fast becoming vain and frivolous, spending hours in empty talk. Frequently she complimented herself on her attributes and talents, read dangerous books and kept questionable company.

Don Alphonso pondered the matter and reached a decision. Teresa would leave for boarding school.

Although at first hostile to the idea of being so restricted, the high-spirited girl eventually calmed down. Formerly surrounded by disreputable companions and foolish reading, Teresa had been heading in the wrong direction. Now she was influenced for the better by wholesome books and friends.

She spent a year and a half with the Augustinian sisters and profited so much from their wise guidance that she began to pray to know God's will in her regard. How would she safely reach salvation? She hoped she wasn't called to the monastic life, but then, she knew she did not want to get married.

Fear of a perpetual commitment paralyzed her in indecision for the next four and a half years. During that time she became the efficient mistress of the de Cepeda estate. But she was not as dedicated to her Faith as she was to her household. She was a mediocre Christian, neither cold nor hot.

Finally, no longer able to stand the turmoil in her soul, Teresa decided to enter the Carmelite convent. Although she felt no attraction whatsoever to that way of life, she knew that it would be the safest and surest way for her to save her soul. However, she had her father to contend with. He adamantly refused permission, and Teresa de Cepeda stood her ground; her honor prevented a retreat once her decision was made, although in a way she rejoiced in her father's refusal.

The human was very strong in Teresa of Avila, as can be seen from her own words: "I could not succeed in overcoming my attachment to my family. My love for my father and brothers was too strong and my love for God very weak and tepid. I had no attraction to the religious life, although I knew I belonged there. Finally I decided and asked my father's permission.

"He told me I could do whatever I wanted when he was dead. Unable to convince him and obtain his blessing, I ran away. When I left, I felt so strong a pull at my heart, I thought the pain would kill me. Not even at death, do I think, I would feel the anguish I felt then. My very bones seemed dislocated. The struggle within me was so great that without God's special grace, I would never have been able to manage." Teresa was then twenty years old.

In the face of the accomplished fact, Don Alphonso gave his consent to his daughter and settled the dowry. The postulant began her existence, which did not prove too difficult. The mitigated rule of the sixteenth-century Carmel left room for a comfortable life which imposed no great demands. Teresa found herself happily spending hours in the parlors, talking with an endless stream of visitors and relatives. These empty, secular conversations soon riddled her prayer life with distractions. She also entertained a dangerous, sentimental affection for one of her cousins, which only added to her spiritual dryness. She desired prayer, yet did not feel worthy to pray because of her love for the things of the world. And instead of detaching herself from these things, she just stopped praying. This precarious situation lasted for some time. Then the intense prayer life of her father and his consequent holy death convinced Teresa of the necessity to again practice mental prayer.

"I returned to prayer," she says in her autobiography, "but I did not cut off the occasions of sin. My life was miserable. I always saw more and more of my faults. On the one hand, God was calling me; on the other, I was following the world. I delighted in the things of God, and I was a prisoner of the world. I was trying to compromise two things — the life of the spirit and the joys of sense."

One day, Teresa was called to the parlor. As she stepped in to greet her guests, her face blanched. She looked beyond her startled guests and stared into the eyes of Someone else they couldn't see. The stern, reproachful gaze of Christ threw her soul into confusion. Teresa blinked hard and mumbled under her breath that she certainly had a very strong imagination, and then commenced her conversation. After the visitors left, Teresa of Avila walked very slowly down the corridor to her cell. She knew she was in the wrong. Her critical self-analysis detected many unworthy motives smouldering under the deceptive ashes of self-love.

The relentless chiding of her conscience cut her deeply. She realized God was trying to tell her something, and she knew exactly what He wanted. Still, she did not make the necessary break.

No one knew of the tremendous struggle going on in her soul except her confessors, one of whom sympathized with her and told her that she was not offending God in any way.

Although she led a very imperfect interior life, Teresa did practice an admirable charity toward her sisters in religion. She never uttered an unkind word about anyone and would never permit anyone to speak ill of others in her presence. She hid her interior turmoil under a mantle of characteristic wit and cheerfulness. She wasn't a bad sister; she just didn't want to go all the way. After all, it was hard to give up *everything!*

Some time later, Teresa passed a picture in the corridor. It was not a new one, nor was it strange in any way. It was in the hall temporarily, on its way to another room. Suddenly Teresa stopped, rooted to the spot. Tears welled up in her eyes as she stared at the picture of Christ covered with the wounds of His passion. Her heart crumbled with remorse as she thought of those wounds and of her ingratitude. She describes her emotion: "I threw myself on my knees before Him, bathed in tears, and I begged Him to strengthen me once and for all, that I might never offend Him in the future."

Eighteen years of mediocrity cannot be overcome in one day. Teresa tried to give up her dangerous, so-called "spiritual friendships," but this caused her such real suffering that she put the whole idea aside. Then God took pity on her. A new confessor, after Christ's own heart, was assigned to the convent. Teresa unburdened her soul to him. She, a lover of truth and candor, told her confessor everything and did exactly what he directed her to do. One day as she was reciting a prayer to the Holy Spirit to ask for the strength needed, she heard these words in the depths of her heart: "Henceforth, it is my will that you no longer converse with men but with angels." Teresa of Jesus knew that her Spouse desired her once and for all to give up her idle moments in the parlor in order to converse with Him and communicate to others what He taught her. Again, she told her confessor of her spiritual experience and obeyed and followed his direction. Finally, she had given in completely to her God!

Speaking of her conversion Teresa says: "The true way for us to submit our wills is through obedience. It cannot be done by reasoning. Our nature and self-love can argue so effectively that reason alone would never get us anywhere. Very often what seems best to us simply because we have no desire to obey, turns out to be an almost ridiculous excuse." Years later, Pope Gregory XV said of Teresa, "She used to say that she might be deceived in discerning visions and revelations, but could never be deceived in obeying superiors."

Filled with the right intention to live a fervent life, Teresa nevertheless became discouraged by the fact that she did not correct herself in one day. Her confessor told her to persevere in her efforts — that God would sanctify her little by little. By repeated falls and renewed efforts the earnest nun

"Whoever wishes to be my follower must deny his very self, take up his cross each day, and follow in my steps."

Luke 9:23

learned that prayer must be founded on the rock of self-denial and mortification. A person who undertakes mental prayer must govern all the senses and cut off, one by one, all excessive attachments.

One of the greatest means Teresa employed to achieve progress in prayer was daily meditation on the passion of Jesus. Deeply moved by our Lord's tender love for her, she always confided entirely in His mercy. She considered the lives of converted saints and reflected on how they had been so quick to repent when our Lord had called them but once; she, instead, had been called so many times and had relapsed so often. She could not get over the great reality of God's goodness towards her. She wrote: "God gives Himself to whoever gives up all things for the love of Him. He excludes no one; He loves all. No one has an excuse, no matter how wicked he may be, since our Lord has been so merciful to me. We must carry the cross if we are to have the joys of heaven that Jesus purchased for us at the price of so much blood and suffering. Oh! How rich one will find himself who leaves all honor and takes pleasure in being humble for the love of God!"

Teresa strove to practice the humility she wrote about. She chose the most humble tasks. Cheerfully and with real energy, she cooked, sewed, swept out the filthiest places in the yard, performed small, unnoticed services for her sisters, and fulfilled many hidden penances and prayers. To external appearances, she was almost the same Teresa, but there had been a total renewal of the inner Teresa.

Holiness does not destroy nature, but perfects it. For twenty years, Teresa worked hard to elevate and supernaturalize her very affectionate disposition and to be always meek and amiable. Hers was a personality which delightfully blended firmness with tenderness, lively wit and imagination with uncommon maturity of judgment.

Under all kinds of trials and inevitable sufferings, she was a picture of constant joy, patience, courage and indomitable strength. Graced with an uncanny sense of humor and intimacy with God, she had all the natural qualities of a leader and yet was a delightful mother to her spiritual daughters. She felt the sufferings of others more than her own. She had indeed come a long way from the spirit of ease and pleasure that had marked her earlier years. Verified in her were her own words: "How great is the good which God works in a soul when He gives it a disposition to pray in earnest though it may not be prepared as it should be. If a person perseveres in spite of sins, temptations, and relapses...our Lord will bring it at last—I am certain of it—to salvation. But one must be courageous in accepting suffering. Trials are a measure of God's love. Merit lies, not in visions and ecstasies, but in doing, suffering, and loving."

Because Teresa had effected her own personal renewal with God's grace, God used her for the genuine renewal of her Order: He bore her up on the wings of mystical prayer and contemplation. But she remained always a realist. It is related that one day, sick and feverish, she bounced along in an open carriage, drenched by rain. Suddenly the carriage lurched forward, dumping its occupants unceremoniously into a mud hole. Dryly, Teresa exclaimed to our Lord, "After so much suffering, Lord, this too!"

"My daughter, this is how I treat my friends," Jesus replied.

"Well," Teresa quipped, "that is why you have so few, my Lord!"

When Teresa of Avila died on October 4, 1582, at the age of sixty-seven, her love for God and souls had reached gigantic proportions. Among her last words, she repeated, "I am a daughter of the Church. ...I am a daughter of the Church!" The good of God's Church had been the power ideal dominating the last years of her earthly existence. The dissensions that took place during her lifetime caused her indescribable pain and alarm. Her intense grief was reflected in the following words: "O my Redeemer! It breaks my heart to see so many souls lose themselves."

Teresa loved the Church passionately and lived for it ardently. She therefore had set about contributing to its holiness by reforming herself. She had made the problems of the Church and humanity the object of her concern and the reasons for her penances.

Eminently human and holy, St. Teresa of Avila knew how to combine prayer and prodigious action for the benefit of the Church and the world.

15

hunted

Sunday, July 16, 1581, dawned calm and warm. Birds twittered and chirped as they basked in the morning sun. The lush, green fields drank in the refreshing dew. This particular July morning gave no indication of the danger about to pounce on unsuspecting humans.

Two horsemen galloped toward Lyford Grange in Berkshire, England. Their steeds pounded the unresisting dust into billowing clouds which hesitated in the air for a moment, then fell to the ground in an expectant silence. The birds ceased warbling; nature grew still and held its breath.

George Eliot and David Jenkins, professional priest-hunters, reined in at the gate of the Lyford Estates. They knew that this was the religious center of the district...the gate was still barred.... It was more than likely that a priest was inside saying Mass.

"Who are you and what is your purpose?" a servant demanded with a suspicious scowl. "Two acquaintances of Thomas Cooper. We understand he is the cook in this manor. We'd like to speak with him." The watchman relaxed and went for the cook. Eliot turned and winked at Jenkins. Presently Cooper came out and greeted Eliot, who explained that he was on his way to Derbyshire.

"Oh, you can wait until after dinner. Come in to the kitchen and have some ale."

Eliot and Jenkins feigned reluctance, but then dismounted. Cooper led the way into the house. After serving the two travelers, the cook approached Eliot and whispered, "Is your companion of our Faith?"

"No," replied Eliot, "but he's an honest man and very favorable toward us." Drawing closer to Eliot, Cooper asked, "Will you go up?"

This was the secret password inviting Eliot to attend Mass. Nodding assent, Eliot accompanied the cook down the hall, into the dining room and through two or three other apartments before entering a large chamber. Mass was already in progress; Eliot hid his delight as he slid into a chair. With simulated devotion, he assisted at the services. His mouth watered with excitement.

The congregation consisted of three nuns, thirty-seven lay people, *and,* not one, but *three* priests, one of whom was none other than Edmund Campion! What a sensational catch! Why, the whole country swarmed with men searching for this priest, and he, George Eliot, had him in the palm of his hand!

After Mass, Campion spoke to the assembly for close to an hour. He poured his very soul into every word. Never before had his eloquence been more compelling. Even Eliot felt a twinge of conscience, that was quickly strangled by the vision of his salary.

His hand strayed to his pocket, ready to whip out credentials. But then, he reflected, it would be better to wait.

Eliot left as fast as he could.

At one o'clock, Mrs. Yate, the mistress of Lyford House, entertained her three priest guests, the three nuns and several lay people who had stayed for dinner. Suddenly, a servant stumbled into the dining room, gasping, "Quick, hide! The house is surrounded. Justice Fettiplace is outside and demands entrance for a search."

Father Campion rose, "My good people," he exclaimed, "perhaps if I surrender, the magistrate will leave you all unharmed."

"Not so," urged Mrs. Yate. "We have many hiding places. There's a good chance of your escaping. Besides, if you surrender, we'll all be ruined."

Quietly, the three priests were led to a small enclosure in the attic. The room, filled with tools, had a sliding panel covering the "priest-hole." Shelves of tools were spread across the panel. Father Campion and his companions lay down side by side on the couch, while Mrs. Yate and a servant placed bread, meat, and wine on the floor. If it were necessary, the priests would have provisions enough to last three or four days. Then the panel was slid into place. Meanwhile, the nuns were already in lay clothes, with their prayerbooks, beads, and holy pictures safely hidden. Mrs. Yate's brother-in-law and two other gentlemen were concealed in the shed.

Almost half an hour passed before Justice Fettiplace was admitted, with the informer, Eliot, walking beside him. Jenkins and a band of searchers milled at their heels.

Indignantly, the occupants of the house demanded the reason for the intrusion. Fettiplace had just unbolted his jaw when Eliot barked, "You were all present at Mass this morning and you are now hiding priests in this house. It is against the law of the realm. It is treasonable."

The justice cleared his throat. He knew Eliot was right about the law, but he had no taste for this priest-hunting business. Suddenly he declared that there would be no search. Eliot protested hotly; he insisted until Fettiplace yielded and the men began to tramp through the house.

Nothing was found. Out at the gate, a disgruntled Eliot confronted Fettiplace; within the manor, the jubilant occupants rejoiced at their escape.

Suddenly, the posse turned around and pounded on the door, shouting for readmittance.

This time, the raid would be led by Eliot. After a few hours, the searchers discovered the three men in the shed. This development lent support to Eliot's claim that something was amiss. Methodically, relentlessly, the hunters stalked their prey. Every corner of the moat and the house was investigated. Bushes were hacked, walls ripped apart, furniture overturned, curtains torn, but nothing revealed the presence of the priests.

Sixty men stayed for supper and slept at various stations in the house. Early the next morning, they resumed the search, but it was futile. Even Eliot finally lost all hope of seizing his "prize." But then, as they were leaving the house, David Jenkins spotted a sliver of light above the staircase landing. A quick swing of the crowbar ripped away the boards to reveal the rear of the "priest-hole" where Edmund Campion and his companions lay, wrapped in silent prayer.

"I've found the traitors," he yelled.

Men flocked to him from all directions and pulled their victims down.

Eliot was elated. He went to court to reap his reward and then proceeded to London with the prisoners. At every stage of the journey large crowds met the procession, and many openly showed their sympathy and love for Father Campion.

"Judas!" several hissed at Eliot. The priest-hunter's initial elation crumbled to dust under the weight of verbal stones. This was almost a march of triumph for Campion! Neither the soldiers nor the magistrates paid any attention to Eliot. Rather, they showed evident dislike for the man.

At last, unable to bear the neglect and scorn any longer, he whined, "Mr. Campion, you regard everyone but me. I know you hate me for what I've done."

"May God forgive you, for thinking that," Father Campion soothed. "I forgive you from my heart." Then he added more solemnly, "And if you repent and come to me for confession, I will absolve you. But I'll have to give you a rather stiff penance."

A swift break away was Eliot's only reply.

Humiliated and paraded through the crowded market streets of London, the priest prisoners arrived at the entrance to the Tower. Campion turned to his guards, thanked them and blessed them. Then the gates slammed shut behind him.

From the end of July to December 1, Campion disappeared from view. These were four months of hidden agony and endurance. When he wasn't being racked or bombarded with merciless, interminable questions under torture, Campion lay in his sunless, isolated cell, wrapped in constant prayer. He remembered his horseback ministry, the days and nights of being sought, pursued, spied upon. He painfully recalled his earlier apostasy as a young scholar, the oath of supremacy he had taken, which had cut him off from the Church and her sacraments for almost twelve years, his ordination as a deacon in the new state religion. And he joyfully reminisced on how he had been brought back to his Faith by reading the works of Saints Augustine, Ambrose, Basil, and the other Fathers of the Church. Convinced of his errors, Campion had then been reconciled to the Church on the continent. Then had followed, in quick succession, his entrance into the Society of Jesus, his intense exercises of self-discipline and prayer and his commission to return to England to administer the sacraments to the faithful who were living under dangerous and oppressive conditions. He had accepted that obedience as his holocaust offering. Long before his tortured body lay in prison, he had made his gift to God and to his countrymen. "As for me all is over...I have made a free oblation of myself to His Divine Majesty both for life and death, and I hope He will give me the grace and strength to perform valiantly. This is all I desire."

Arriving on England's shores, Campion had passed through the countryside disguised as a jeweler. In only one month, he had visited over fifty or more homes, saying Mass and administering the sacraments to sorely oppressed Catholics. There had followed another six months of hiding, running, hair-splitting escapes and fatiguing work that sapped Campion's strength. Each time it was the same: arrive at a house as a friend or relative of known Catholics living there; accept hospitality in a hidden section of the house; change into priestly vestments, hear confessions far into the night and perhaps preach, then say Mass very early and leave without the rest of the household knowing his true identity. Noblemen and women, commoners and servants — all assembled secretively, risking positions, property and life to rejuvenate their thirsting spirits. Because of severe penalties levied on them, many had been dragged down to the depths of destitution. Despair had been fired with rebellion. In his early days of priestly ministry in England, Father Campion had written of his flock's plight: "The faithful speak of nothing but death, flight, prison or ruination of families and friends. They are impoverished to the verge of ruin by the fines imposed on them for hearing Mass, harboring priests, and failing to attend state religion services."

After nine months of again having opportunities to receive the sacraments, the faithful no longer complained of lengthy services, as they had in the past. Driven back to the life of the catacombs, the Church in England was recovering the very spirit of the early Christians. Campion's stirring eloquence, exuberant faith, and daring courage had brought the English new hope and vitality. By their lives Campion and other heroic priests had showed that despair and rebellion need not be the only way to react to oppression. Persecution, be it subtle or violent—could be met with heroism and even joyful martyrdom for the love of God.

Campion had known, of course, that although the faith of the people flourished, the paid informers and priest-hunters were never lacking. Hence, he wrote: "I cannot long escape the hands of the enemy. They have so many eyes, so many tongues, so many scouts and tricks. I am ridiculously dressed and often change my name.... But there will always be men in England who will care for their own salvation and the salvation of others. The Church here will never fail as long as there are devoted shepherds to tend their flocks and snatch them from the devil, no matter how ferociously he roars."

As the last hours of his life ebbed away, Campion recalled the reason for all his present torture and suffering. He had written to the court over a year before: "Daily, many innocent hands are lifted up to heaven for you by English students beyond the seas. They are gathering virtue and sufficient knowledge to help you and are determined never to give you up as lost; either they will win you to heaven or die upon your pikes.... Know that we Jesuits shall cheerfully carry the cross you shall lay upon us and never despair of your recovery—as long as we have a man left to enjoy your gallows or to be racked with your torments or consumed in your prisons. We've weighed the scales, the enterprise is begun; such were the conditions under which the Faith was sown in England; such will be the condition for restoring it. It is of God. It cannot be withstood. And if my offers be refused and my efforts thwarted, and if after running thousands of miles for your good I shall be rewarded with torments—I, Campion, have no more to say than to recommend your case and mine to God. At least, may we be friends in heaven through God's grace. There all injuries shall be forgotten."

During the last eleven days of his life, Edmund Campion was chained. Fearful of reprisals, Eliot, the man responsible for Campion's imprisonment and torture, went to visit the heroic priest.

Father Edmund reassured Eliot that his life was not in danger. He added that if the informer was still afraid he knew of someone on the continent who would give him shelter.

Campion's guard, Delahays, was present at the conversation. Deeply moved by Father Campion's love and forgiveness toward Eliot, he was converted and later entered the Church.

Father Edmund prayed and fasted and knelt through the last two nights. On December 1, 1581, after being dragged behind a horse through the mud, Edmund Campion stood in a cart beneath the gallows on Tyburn Hill and cried out, "We are a spectacle to God and men." He tried to talk, but the crowd shouted him down. More noise followed as Campion silently prayed. His last words were: "I have prayed for and do so now for my queen and your queen, whom I have not offended. May God grant her a long and quiet reign, in all prosperity." The noose had been placed about his neck, and the cart was now drawn from under him.

The martyred saint was forty-two.

Campion and so many like him came with gaiety among a people where hope was dead. Men with light hearts, they were tender, compassionate and dedicated. They followed holiness though it led them through bitter ways to poverty, disgrace, exile, imprisonment and death. Their flock caught their fire and burned brightly for future generations, trusting in the word of God:

"My son, when you come to serve the Lord,
    prepare yourself for trials.
Be sincere of heart and steadfast,
    undisturbed in time of adversity.
Cling to him, forsake him not;
    thus will your future be great.
Accept whatever befalls you,
    in crushing misfortune be patient;
For in fire gold is tested,
    and worthy men in the crucible of humiliation.
Trust God and he will help you....
Compassionate and merciful is the Lord;
    he forgives sins, he saves in time of trouble."
    (Sir. 2:1-6, 11)

16

pearl
of
York

It was 8:00 in the morning of March 25, 1586. The sun already shone brightly, warming the dark, narrow streets of York, England. The city, which generally bustled with activity, was unusually silent. Most of the merchants' shops were still shuttered and small groups of people huddled in doorways discussing the events about to take place.

There was one shop that hadn't been open for business for two or three weeks—a butcher shop located on a street called Shambles. Its proprietors? John and Margaret Clitherow, a typical married couple. The large house adjoining the establishment, usually filled with children's laughter and servants' chatter, stood silent. Only a few muffled sobs had broken the quiet of the past five days.

Meanwhile, in another part of town, the jingling of keys and the clanking of iron bars rudely interrupted the quiet prayer of a young Englishwoman, barely turned thirty.

"Come away, Mrs. Clitherow."

Not for all the money in England would Margaret Clitherow have refused that rough invitation.

Escorted by a band of armed soldiers, Margaret passed through the dark, dungeon-lined hallways. She stumbled up the long flight of stairs and instinctively raised her hands to her eyes. After spending such a long time in semi-darkness, she found the brightness of daylight startling.

Her guards brutally pushed her forward, hoping to put a quick end to all this nonsense which was depriving them of half a day at the local tavern.

The heavy, oaken door of Ouse Bridge prison closed behind Margaret and her escorts, and she began her barefoot trudge down the muddy streets. People pressed in on the little band from all sides, in order to bid Margaret a last farewell. When they reached the place of torture called Tollbooth, they were greeted by the execution team, which included four women and eight men, chosen from the lowest rung of society. Those who had sentenced Margaret were nowhere in sight. They had hired others to perform this cruel job in their stead.

Margaret was led into the small, grey stone structure and brought down to a torture chamber in the basement.

A few moments were allowed her for prayer. Then she was commanded, "Mrs. Clitherow, you must remember and confess that you die for treason."

"No," came the staunch refusal. "I die for the love of my Lord Jesus."

At this, the executioners wreaked their fury on the frail victim. They stripped her and threw her down on a sharp stone. Next, they placed a heavy door upon her body and bound her arms outward in the form of a cross. Finally, they lowered up to eight hundred pounds of weights onto the door.

Margaret's last audible words were, "Jesus! Jesus! Jesus! Have mercy on me." Then there was silence. In fifteen minutes the ordeal was over and Margaret Clitherow entered into everlasting happiness.

Margaret Clitherow, now known as "the Pearl of York," was born in 1556. It was the Tudor era, an age marked by joviality and tragedy, abundance and want, culture and barbarism. It was an age of contradictions, and Margaret's life was to be tinged with them.

Her father, Thomas Middleton, a craftsman and candlemaker, ran a booming business in those days when there were no gas and electricity. He also enjoyed the prestige of being warden of the Church of St. Martin on Coney Street. The minister and church assembly held all the Middletons in high regard.

At a time when girls were usually married between fourteen and sixteen, Margaret was even more outgoing than most young people. Although she loved her mother and gave much of her time to domestic affairs, she was no less a socialite and spent the remaining portion of her time at the dances and banquets so characteristic of Elizabethan England.

In May of 1567, however, sorrow struck the Middleton household. Brought to his grave by the gout, Margaret's much-loved father was laid to rest in the Church of St. Martin. Margaret had just turned eleven.

Less than five months later, to everyone's shock and dismay, Thomas' widow, Jane, married again. Henry May, an innkeeper, was Margaret's new stepfather. He had been only too happy to marry the rich widow of Thomas Middleton. Her money would enable him to rise to the high offices of the city. In fact, at the time of Margaret's death, May would hold the office of Lord Mayor, the highest position in York.

Margaret was a "good" young woman, but certainly not overly pious. The most she did in the way of religion was attend weekly church services with her mother.

Sometime in late 1570 or early 1571, Mr. May began to look for a suitable husband for his stepdaughter. His choice fell on John Clitherow, a tradesman of thirty-one. He was a wealthy butcher, highly esteemed in York. Originally a Catholic, he had fallen away from his Faith as he had risen in the community. John's business was both wholesale and retail, and it is likely that Henry May procured the meat for his inns from his future son-in-law.

John and Margaret were married in grand style on July 1, 1571, and they took up residence in a large, beautiful Tudor house on Shambles Street. John's first wife, Matilda, had died shortly after the birth of their second child. Therefore, when Margaret arrived at her new home, two little toddlers were waiting for her. She loved and cherished them with all the affection of a real mother.

So, at fifteen, Margaret found herself the wife of a well-to-do butcher. Along with all her other domestic duties, she was expected to oversee and help in the butcher shop and direct a large household of servants, most of whom were probably older than herself. John was often away on trips involving the wholesale side of his business, and the full responsibility of home and business fell on Margaret's unusually mature shoulders.

It was in this fashion that life continued in the stately house on Shambles Street, with new members being added to the Clitherow family from time to time. John and Margaret appeared to be a perfect match. Their mutual love grew with the passing of the years.

Then, in 1574, something happened that turned the tide in Margaret's hitherto uneventful life. A number of Catholic priests arrived in York. They had been trained at Douay in Flanders and were returning to England in order to minister to the needs of the faithful.

The priests could not have come at a worse time. A law had been passed banning the celebration of Mass and ordering that anyone caught giving hospitality to priests was to be taken into custody.

Observing the heroic constancy of many of her Catholic friends under these trying circumstances, Margaret became aware of much that she had neither known nor understood about Catholics before.

After a time, Margaret was received into the Catholic Church and began to practice the Faith as best she could under the circumstances.

She spent the remaining years of her life in and out of prison. Despite the fact that John Clitherow never returned to Catholicism, he willingly paid heavy fines in order to release his dear wife whenever she was arrested for practicing her religion. For John, no fine, no matter how heavy, was comparable to the treasure of his beautiful Margaret. But Margaret knew that sooner or later she would return to prison for the last time.

On June 12, 1585, her mother died, and on January 15, 1586, her stepfather, Henry May, was appointed Lord Mayor of York. May was determined to make Margaret give up her new way of life. Her prayers, fastings, and "Catholic reputation" were ruining his own, he felt. At least, they were causing him much embarrassment. He called for a raid on her home. The searchers found no priest, so they threatened a small group of children who had come to the

Clitherow house for school. "If you don't show us where Mrs. Clitherow hides priests, we'll beat you!"

One tiny Flemish lad succumbed to his dreadful fear and led the soldiers to the room where Margaret kept priestly vestments and various altar appointments. At once Margaret was seized and thrown into prison.

Of all her friends, no one appeared in her defense at the trial. Only one Puritan preacher, the Reverend Mr. Wigginton, fearlessly spoke out in her behalf. He told the judge, "My Lord, take heed to what you do. You sit here to do justice; this case is touching death and life. Therefore, look to it, my Lord; this is a serious matter."

The judge replied, "I may do it by law."

"By what law?" asked the minister.

"By the law of the country."

"That may well be," replied the good preacher, "but you cannot do it by God's law."

Although Margaret faced death calmly, she feared greatly for her husband and children. "As for my husband," she replied, "know that I love him next to God in this world, and I have care over my children, as a mother ought to have; I have done my duty to them to bring them up in the fear of God, and so I trust now that I am discharged of them. And for this cause I am willing to offer them freely to the God that sent them to me, rather than yield one jot from faith."

As the day of her execution drew near, Margaret prayed, fasted and did penance. She begged her friends to do the same for her. "The flesh is frail," she repeated several times before her death, always adding, "but I trust in my Lord Jesus, that He will give me strength to bear all the troubles and torments which shall be laid upon me for His sake."

And she received from the Lord the strength she needed. In the hour of trial, she was *not* found wanting in courage.

After Margaret's death, her mangled body was thrown into a dunghill, where a small group of Catholics found it six weeks later. To their amazement, it was completely incorrupt. They gave the body a reverent burial, after severing one hand from it to keep as a relic. The secret of her burial place was guarded so well that soon all knowledge of its whereabouts was lost completely.

In our own times, Mass is celebrated daily at Margaret's house on Shambles Street and she is venerated as St. Margaret Clitherow, Martyr—Pearl of York.

17

convicted
of
love

The time was September, 1636, and the place was London—a city ravaged by a merciless killer—the plague. A lone figure made his way down the narrow streets lined with squashed, wooden tenements. On his long robe an insignia could be seen, and in his hand a white rod gave warning. No one was to come near him. He had been in contact with plague victims.

His steps echoed on the cobblestones as he plowed through piled-up rubbish and skirted the glowing embers of "medicinal" bonfires. He reached a tenement of St. Giles-in-the-Fields. This suburb was a byword for squalor. Two city officials stood guard. Recognizing the man who approached, they unlocked the padlock of the only entrance to the house and allowed him in. Then the door was pulled shut again.

Inside, the foul air, heavy with smoke and gases, choked and blinded Father Henry Morse. He gasped a moment and wiped the tears from his stinging eyes. A woman staggered over to him, took his hat and led him to her husband's sickbed. One look was sufficient for Father Morse to know that time was limited.

Pulling a stole from under his cassock, he bent over the dying man to hear his last confession and anoint him. As he did so, his face blanched. He was especially sensitive to the odors of the plague victims. Due to the city's ordinances, all infected homes were shut up like sealed tombs, enclosing sick and healthy alike. Windows were tightly fastened and even keyholes blocked. Daily, Morse would blame himself for lack of courage in administering the sacraments to the sick and pushed himself on. Lifting the head of this dying man, Father Henry cradled it in his arms until the plague victim breathed his last. Morse then arranged the body and handed a small pouch of money to the widow. As silently as he had come, Father Henry left. He was a bit more weary, perhaps, but also happier. He had helped another person cross the threshold of heaven.

On returning to his lodgings that night, Father Morse felt a strange fatigue crippling his muscles. He shivered uncontrollably as his head spun with giddiness. The disease gripped him. Doctor Thomas Turner was immediately summoned. He prescribed nightly sweats. During the daytime, Father Henry would continue to work. The needs and the numbers of the sick didn't allow for rest. He and another priest, Father Southworth, were the only two dedicated to the distribution of alms and administration of the sacraments to the thousands of afflicted Catholics of London. Slowly, very slowly, Father Morse regained sufficient strength to resume his nightly calls.

Day after day, night after night, he worked on. He had far from recovered. But he would not allow himself any time for convalescence. Then, to his ill health and the burden of work was added yet more. Father Southworth was arrested by "priest-hunters" and confined to prison. This left Father Morse all alone.

The plague's grip on the devastated city tightened. Deaths reached an all-time high. In November, 1636, although the death rate slumped off somewhat, Father Morse's work did not become easier. Again he fell ill. And it seemed that this time death would claim its victim.

When the superior of the London Jesuit Fathers heard about Father Morse's relapse, he wrote to him and ordered him to stop all his work for the plague-stricken and to rest until he had completely recovered. Meanwhile, all the brethren in England were praying for him.

Morse raised himself up on his elbow and held the letter up to the flame for more light. Doctor Turner and a colleague, Doctor More, stood by. Father Henry's body, covered with sores, shook with a violent fever that could momentarily snuff out his life. Suddenly, the priest dropped the letter. Eyes glistening with awe and joy, he exclaimed, "Doctor Turner, something marvelous has just happened! The crisis has passed. I'm no longer in danger of death. I'm getting well!"

Turner's medical eye noted the change. But the pustules on Morse's body would still have to be lanced, and Father didn't want the doctor to take the risk to his own life.

"I must do it," Turner protested. "I know I'm taking a chance, but isn't that what you've been doing every night and day for months?"

After the operation, the doctor nursed the self-sacrificing Jesuit for several days. Then, still very weak and shaky, Morse resumed his errands of mercy. There were about four hundred and eighty Catholic families to help—approximately two or three thousand people. Morse served not only them but also anyone else who needed help, regardless of religious affiliation. His great kindness and complete self-effacement won many converts to the Church. It was reported that as many as five hundred persons were received into the Church by Father Henry Morse during the years of the plague. But as his name became great and the number of converts grew so did the zeal of grasping "priest-hunters."

One day that November, a vengeful woman reported Morse as a priest performing priestly duties — something completely against the law of the realm. The next day, as Father Henry was about to enter a house to give Holy Communion to the sick, a constable stepped out of the shadows and arrested him. But the constable liked Father Morse and admired this man who heroically served the sick when so many others didn't care or bother. He was plainly irritated that the law had been invoked against the dedicated clergyman. After half a day, Morse's case was dismissed and he was again a free man.

Shortly afterward, Father Henry was again summoned to the pest house in St. Giles-in-the-Fields. As he approached a filthy bed, every natural instinct in him revolted. A young man lay there, full of plague spots and sores on his ears, lips and forehead. Father Morse sat on the edge of the bed and forced himself to place his ear close to the man's lips so as to hear the barely audible voice. The youth had contracted a bigamous marriage and he found it hard to confess it and to have the necessary sorrow. Morse lavished every act of kindness on the youth, urging him to repentance. He offered up his own act of self-denial to win grace for the poor wretch. Suddenly the young man broke out into heart-rending sobs. He had received God's mercy! Morse anointed him and also brought his wife back to the Church.

Right after Christmas, the priest was once more arrested and held, then confined to Newgate Prison the following March. Overcrowded, Newgate was a breeding place for the plague. After being led up three flights of stone-slab steps, Morse entered a large room with other prisoners. The bars of the windows were as thick as a man's wrist. Beds were nothing else but boards scantily covered with a few feathers. The tables and chairs had obviously been pulled out from some age of the ancient past. Morse remained at Newgate for four weeks. He moved among the criminals of all classes, hearing confessions, exhorting and giving Holy Communion —always secretly. He had done the same during his previous imprisonments—the first in New Prison and the second in York Jail—each of which had lasted four years. In fact, it is said that while Father Morse was in York every criminal, before being led to execution, had been brought into the Church through his gentle and persevering endeavors.

On April 22, 1637, Morse was called to trial. He was allowed no defense attorney, but aptly defended himself, since he had been a lawyer before his conversion and ordination in the early 1620's. The following day, back at Newgate Prison, Father Henry pronounced his final vows as a Jesuit. On April 26, he was summoned to court. Morse wrote, "I therefore set my thoughts on heaven and braced myself to receive my sentence. But it was not pronounced. The king had instructed the court to defer my sentence. I was led back to prison."

But prison confinement proved too much. He had contracted the plague again and soon was near death. He wrote a personal letter to King Charles I and asked to be released so as to regain his health. The letter was effective. On June 17, Father Morse was released and placed under the king's direct protection.

Father Henry completely recovered and worked for two more years until he was again arrested by his old enemies. He escaped over to the continent and became a chaplain to the English troops there. He served in this capacity for several years, until his return to London in 1643. Always he labored ceaselessly, a remarkable example to his brethren, doing all that was asked of a most faithful and hard-working priest.

In England Morse was too famous to escape detection. Again he was arrested and confined to Newgate Prison. There was no trial, only the death sentence. A charge against him read: "Convicted of priesthood."

Led back to prison, Morse awaited his execution. During the last four days of Father Henry's life, visitors from every class poured into the prison. Some came out of curiosity, others wanted to ask his prayers or deliver some message from their sick relatives. They took no pains to hide the fact that they were Catholics. They had come to pay their respects to a man who was a hero for them. Especially on the last night before Morse died, hundreds came from the first hours of the day to the last hours of night, to congratulate him on the victory at hand, and to beg his prayers of intercession for themselves and for their suffering country. Ambassadors from every major nation in Europe came to visit the heroic priest.

That last night he did not sleep. Rather, he received visitors until four o'clock in the morning, as though he had nothing in the world to worry about except the interests of each individual that came to him. After Father Henry said Mass, he recited his Breviary and then visited all the prisoners with such serenity and gentleness that he amazed everyone.

At nine o'clock, the sheriff came to take the prisoner to execution. Father Morse fell on his knees, joined his hands in prayer and thanked God in a loud voice. He then lay down on the hurdle that would drag him to Tyburn Hill Gallows. When they were but a few yards from Tyburn, a richly decorated coach drew up alongside the hurdle. The Marquis de Sabran dismounted, stepped into the muddy road, and bending his knees begged for Father Morse's blessing.

An hour later, heaven boasted of a new citizen, and England had obtained a new intercessor. It was 1645, the fiftieth year of Saint Henry Morse's earthly life and the dawn of his eternal life.

18

the
holy
black

"Say, Ben!" a voice raised itself above the clamor of the hot Sicilian market place. It caught the attention of a burley young man struggling through the crowd with twin sacks of grain slung over each shoulder. Benedict stopped and smiled broadly as he recognized Antonio, a neighboring farmer.

"What can I do for you, Tony?" he returned, as the smaller man side-stepped to avoid a passing cart before arriving at Benedict's side.

"I hear you've got yourself a sturdy team of oxen that you're hiring out. You know that meadow on the northern edge of my farm? I'd like to get it plowed in time for planting, and I could use your help."

Benedict's smile broadened, if that were possible. "Sure. How about the day after tomorrow, Tony? I have to finish up a few things for Signor Manasseri, and then I'll be able to come."

161

"Agreed," Tony grinned. "You sure do like that Manasseri, don't you?" he continued, shaking his head, "even though he still owns your mother and father.... Can't understand it.... Well, be seeing you Wednesday, then," the farmer concluded as he clapped Benedict on the back and moved on his way.

He can't understand the way I feel about Signor Manasseri? Benedict wondered. Why, the master is the kindest slave owner in all of Sicily! That should be reason enough! It was because of him that Benedict even *had* a yolk of oxen in the first place. At this thought, a renewed warmth welled up inside him.

Christopher and Diana, Benedict's parents, had been brought from Ethiopia many years before and sold to Signor Manasseri as slaves. Their owner, however, had treated the Christian couple well from the very beginning; he had even given his word that their first son, born in 1526, would be given his freedom when he turned fourteen. The unbelievable promise had been kept, and though at first Benedict had remained with his parents working in the vineyards, he had begun to earn wages for his labors. The added income, small though it was, eased the family's poverty somewhat. Then the oxen had come — bought with his savings — this was simply the ultimate for the young black.

Wednesday came. A clear, still sunrise lightened the eastern sky and promised plenty of hot, dry sun. Benedict whistled as he walked the team toward Antonio's farm. The prospect of a good day of satisfying hard work made him impatient to begin; he goaded the oxen a little to hasten their steps.

"Hey, fellas, here comes Big Black Ben!" A familiar shout, trembling in mock fear, cut off Ben's tune abruptly.

A burst of laughter followed and the group of young farm hands with whom Benedict often worked joined him as they headed for the northern meadow....

The plowing and clearing progressed well, and by mid-morning nearly a quarter of the area lay in rich, dark furrows. The boys were in high spirits today, and at their break for water a round of slap-happy jokes and fun-poking began. Usually they teased good-naturedly, even though they always aimed at the big, gentle Ben. But today, in their lightheaded exhilaration, the boys became almost cruel.

Benedict listened at first, but as the barrage grew heavier he tried not to. He knew that they really did not mean what they were saying about his slave father, his color and origin. They were just having a good time, Ben thought, so why not let them? The field, however, still lay mostly untilled, covered with plenty of saplings and underbrush to be cleared. Ben was almost ready to suggest that they go back to work, when an austere, grey-haired figure strode into their group from behind a hedge.

"You empty-headed fools!" he shouted. The boys stopped in mid-sentence. They recognized Jerome Lanza, a well-known hermit and holy man of the area.

"I've been listening quite long enough to your derision." Slowly, intently, Lanza gazed into each of the now sheepish faces. "This young man will be a religious before long," he went on. Noting their surprise, he added, "Yes, this Benedict whom you taunt for his lowliness. And in a few years he will also be famous and sought after." The hermit stood calmly for a full minute more, his gaze making one last circuit of the ring of faces. Then he turned quietly and walked toward the road. Nothing could be heard but the pebbles crunching under his sandals.

Then there was an embarrassed shuffling of feet and the clink and scrape of tools being gathered.

Benedict clucked to the team and headed them back onto the meadow. Actually he was nearly as surprised at Jerome's thunderous intervention and prophecy as the others.

Me a religious? he thought. I know next to nothing about the things of God—only how to love and trust Him. And I have nothing to offer Him except myself.... Thoughtful furrows, nearly as deep as those his plow made, crowded Benedict's brow. What does God want of me? he wondered.

A few days passed. Then, as suddenly as before, Lanza was beside him again, urging Benedict to follow God's call.

"But," began the younger man, "I have nothing to offer..." and he recounted his thoughts of the first day. The hermit's grey whiskers parted in a wise smile. "You have yourself, Ben, your strength and your life. More than that no one can give and more than your all the Lord does not ask."

A whirring of wings and a startled bird's cry broke the early quiet of the hillside, and heralded the approach of someone to the hermitage of Jerome Lanza and his companions. That someone was broad shouldered and black—Benedict was "coming home." He quickly became one with the solitaries, and poured every ounce of himself into serving God and his brothers.

Several times in the years that followed, the group was required to change its location. The actual moving was simple, since the hermits had very little to move except themselves. But each new site did call for a good deal of labor—forested areas had to be cleared and small huts built for each of the men. It was always Benedict who seemed to be everywhere at once. He spoke little; *deeds* were his conversation,

"I shall walk before the Lord in the lands of the living."

Psalm 116:9

and he made sure everyone else was taken care of before he dealt with his own needs.

One particular time, Brother Jerome stopped him as he dragged two large logs across the clearing of their newest home.

"Where are you going, Brother Benedict? Your hut will be at the other end won't it?"

"Oh yes," Benedict nodded in reply. "But you see, Brother Francis needs a little help getting his built. He wasn't too well this morning, and being older.... Then I promised Brother Joseph that I'd help him with splitting that large tree he has, and with fixing his roof. And then...."

Jerome held up his hand, smiling. "Okay, Benedict. But will you have a roof over your own head tonight?"

"I'll do my best, Brother," Benedict promised, "but where I sleep tonight doesn't really matter."

Lanza was up late that night. As he made his way back to his own corner of the compound, he nearly tripped over a pair of feet, protruding from what seemed to be a heap of branches. Peering more intently into the darkness, Jerome could make out the full form of a peacefully sleeping Brother Benedict. Over his head was his "roof" — several large branches leaned against the trunk of a tree to form a sort of tent.

Jerome reached down to shake the younger man and invite him to his own hut for the rest of the night. But then he pulled back. That would be the very last thing Brother Benedict would want, the older hermit reflected. God bless him! He's always so full of thought for everyone else that he just simply forgets the minor details, like himself!

The final move of the small community brought them to the craggy slopes of Mt. Pellegrino near Palermo. They had just settled down, when the

Lord asked one last sacrifice of them. Brother Jerome died. It was a shock to each and every one of the hermits. Lanza had been a superior and father to them since the first days they had gathered. Benedict, especially, was struck. How much good this man of God had done for him; why Benedict owed his very vocation to him! And now, he thought, as they silently left the burial grounds, now someone will have to try to take his place—a nearly impossible task!

Benedict decided then and there to pray for and be as loyal as possible to the successor. It is never easy to fill a founder's shoes.

The group met to select a new superior. There was very little discussion; it was almost as if there had been some sort of previous agreement. Benedict wondered where *he* had been, as he had no inkling of any planning. He was brought back from his reverie abruptly as he heard his own name being called. What was going on? Perhaps they needed something?

"Brother Benedict," Brother Francis repeated. "We've chosen you to be our superior. Do you consent?"

Disbelief etched itself into every feature of the ebony face. "This is no time for jokes, Brother Francis," he replied. "What is it that you really need?"

It took quite a bit of talking to convince him that they meant what they said, and even when he *did* realize their sincerity, Benedict did not see how he could *possibly* accept. "But I've had no schooling," he protested, "and not much experience. And besides —I have trouble enough guiding myself! How can you expect me to guide others well?" He tried every angle, but the brothers were sure their choice had been a good one.

"All right," he finally sighed. "All things are possible to him who trusts in God.... I will simply trust."

This became the key to his every problem — trust in God. And all things did become possible. Though every step of the way required abundant prayer and plenty of effort on his own part, God did work marvels through His Moor. Benedict's leadership was wise and steady; once he had taken on the burden of authority, he carried it simply, uncomplainingly and well.

Relief, however, came from an unexpected quarter. In 1562, Pope Pius IV decreed that all hermits such as Benedict's group were to disband or join one of the already established religious orders. Benedict chose the Friars Minor of the Observance; he had always admired St. Francis' simplicity and adherence to the Gospel life. Near Palermo was the monastery of St. Mary, where he was readily accepted as a lay brother and assigned to the kitchen.

Finally, Benedict thought, a hidden duty and a hidden life! There would be all sorts of opportunities to serve the Lord in others here as cook. And serve he did. He was up before dawn, starting the fire in the kitchen hearth and preparing a good, hot breakfast for the brothers. And as always he remembered and did the hundred little things that go into thoughtfulness in daily living.

Growing daily in selfless love for his neighbor, Benedict also drew closer to the Father of all. He placed his trust in Him more completely every day — and marvelous things began happening. There was that unexplainable sack of fresh bread which the novice helping in kitchen found right after Brother Benedict had given away their last loaf to a beggar at the door. And there was Brother Elias' arthritis — once it had so crippled his knees that he could barely walk to chapel. Brother Benedict had cared for him with nightly hotpacks for only a week, and his legs were like new....

For Benedict these were all merely part of trust—trust so clear and childlike that the Lord couldn't help but answer. In fact, the friar was surprised at the "fuss" people made over these events and shied away from special recognition. But goodness is like the Gospel's "city on a mountain top"—it cannot be hidden. The other brothers watched and noted it well.

Nearly sixteen years had passed since Benedict had come to St. Mary's, when he again heard those dreaded words, "We have chosen you as our superior, Brother...." Again Benedict tried to convince his confreres how ill-suited he was for the office—he could neither read nor write and was only a lay brother.... But under obedience he was obliged to accept, and he did. It was a time of the turmoil of reform and renewal, and an especially wise superior was required. The brothers of St. Mary's found in Benedict abundant wisdom and kindness.

Both in his years as superior, and later as cook, novice master and vicar of the monastery, Brother Benedict never lost his knack for selfless kindness and concern. The monastery at Palermo became the object of a veritable pilgrimage of constant visitors. All of Sicily knew it could count on Brother Benedict's ready welcome and open hand. Though he never refused to see anyone who asked for him, he still shrank from all marks of respect and publicity. He even got to the point of having to travel at night to avoid being recognized and surrounded by a crowd of well-meaning villagers.

Benedict's gnarled hands seemed ageless and tireless in their distribution of aid—always the fruit of his trust in God. There was such a timeless quality about him that it was at first puzzling and then unbelievable when one morning in 1589 Brother Benedict did not arrive in chapel for Mass. He died later that day, as peacefully and quietly as he had lived. The wake of shock at his death gave way to grateful remembrance and prayers. This patron of the North American Negro left as a legacy of his life the words of the Psalmist:

"I believed, even when I said,
  'I am greatly afflicted';
I shall walk before the Lord
  in the lands of the living" (Ps. 116:10, 9).

19

"he
played
the
fool"

A long, winding procession of three thousand people made its way through the streets of Rome in the mid 1550's. Pilgrimages in general were not strange, but this *was* a strange pilgrimage. The sermons and Mass that began it were followed by music and magnificent choral singing. Midway along the route, everyone stopped at a certain estate, sat on the grass and ate a simple picnic breakfast. Then more music and singing followed, until the pilgrimage terminated. Men desire happiness, and they can be drawn to God in joy.

These pilgrimages were to do just that. Their founder had introduced an element of innocent gaiety into them in order to lead the young away from the licentious Mardi Gras carnivals.

Who was this strange, little man behind the pilgrimages — this man with snow-white beard and sparkling blue eyes? The city of Rome had never really been the same since his appearance in the squares, shops, schools and banks, back in 1538.

From the beginning, Philip Neri had shown an engaging personality. He would strike up a conversation with anyone he met. Beginning with, "Well, my good friend, when shall we start to do some good?" he would continue talking about God and spiritual matters. Won by his vivacity, a large group of teen-agers, business men, paupers, nobles, and crafts-men often followed him to his bare room to continue their conversations with him and pray together.

These spiritual conversations quickly led to the desire to lead better lives, and Philip urged his friends to go to confession, for a good confession was the beginning of a reformed life. Through the act of confession they would secure that all-important humility which is so necessary.

When Philip began his career of winning souls to God, he had no intentions of becoming a priest. But his confessor—a very holy man himself—insisted. Philip gave in although he felt his unworthiness keenly. Now, besides being a friend and confidant he was also a confessor, and his work grew and grew.

Father Philip Neri was not one to abide by the usual, the conventional, the "proper" way to do things. He followed one course alone—improvisation and spontaneity.

Word of the meetings at the "oratory," as it was called, spread rapidly throughout Rome. Many distinguished personages came to see and hear for themselves. And then they joined. Among these were musicians and great singers, whom Philip invited to lend moments of relaxation between the sessions of instructions.

Orazio Griffi, a papal singer, wrote the fol-lowing in regard to Neri's work: "There couldn't have been an easier or more effective way of exciting souls to a perfect love and fear of God than those daily reflections on the hatefulness of sin, the punishments of hell, the beauty of holiness, and eternal happiness. In this way, people were disposed to do penance, urged to receive Holy Communion often, and moved to perform works of charity. And this was your work, Blessed Philip.... In order to achieve your zealous purpose and attract sinners to the oratory you used music and had us sing sacred songs. In this way you lured the people by the singing and the sermons to desire and resolve to lead good lives. Some came to the oratory only for the music, but then they were touched by the sermons and were converted to God with great fervor."

But all was not sweet for Philip; there were many in Rome who suspected him of trying to form a new sect, or of aiming for high positions in the Church, and of course, there were those who envied him for the good he was doing. He was persecuted by several and misunderstood even by other saints of the time. At one point, things got so bad that one day at Mass when he raised the Sacred Host, Philip cried out to the Lord, "O good Jesus, why is it that You don't hear me, and why is my soul disturbed by thoughts of anger and impatience?"

"You ask me for patience?" Christ answered in the depths of his soul. "I give it to you now, on the condition that if you really desire it, you earn it by fighting these temptations."

At another time, Neri thought of abandoning his work in Rome and going to Milan, or to India as a missionary. But he was told that his India would be Rome.

Philip Neri was primarily a confessor, a man accessible to all at any time of the day or night. From daybreak to noon he stayed in church to hear confessions. If no penitents came, he would remain near the confessional and pray, read, or say his office or recite the rosary. Every now and then he would go outside and walk up and down in front of the church so people would know that a priest was available. And many times he heard confessions into the wee hours of the morning.

Years later, when he was old and sick and his disciples begged him not to tire himself out by hearing so many confessions, he retorted, "I tell you that those of my penitents who are now most spiritual are the very ones I gained to the Lord by being always accessible, even at night."

He loved children and the young people and did all he could to keep them away from sin. He would willingly join in games because by playing with them he knew he was serving God in his young friends. "The young can chop wood on my back," he said, "as long as they do not sin."

He could be severe and stern with the advanced at times, but most tender and compassionate with the weak and sinners. He used to say, "If you wish to go to extremes, let it be in gentleness, patience, humility, and charity." Philip's program for the conversion of sinners and the cultivation of good, fervent Christians was the same as that of St. Colombini: "Speak constantly of Jesus. Cultivate charity towards all creatures. Practice mortification."

He insisted on humility and cheerfulness. Convinced that the gloomy could make no headway in the spiritual life, he said, "I want you never to commit sin but to be always gay and joyful-hearted. A cheerful and glad spirit reaches perfection much more readily than a melancholy spirit."

He liked people to laugh and joke—a gay spirit was to him a sign of innocence. Self-love is the cause of most unhappiness; egotists are invariably miserable. Joy is one of the most rapid means to holiness. Humility is the source of joy. The more completely a man is detached, the greater his happiness.

In order to bring about this humility in his penitents, Philip would prescribe extraordinary humiliations, ludicrous ones that would help his disciples make fools of themselves for the love of God as he himself did. In fact, the more he found himself esteemed by men, the more Father Neri made himself ridiculous. His oratory became known as the school of Christian mirth.

There were no limits to how far Philip would go to make others think less of him. He would go out to meet great personages fantastically dressed, wearing his clothes inside-out, half-shaven, or wearing long white shoes. Sometimes he would strut around Rome in furs given to him by a cardinal to make people think he was vain. On other occasions, he would walk in the streets with a handful of brooms and stop once in a while to smell them and pretend to enjoy the fragrant scent! He would do anything to make people think he was foolish. But common sense always lay under all of Philip's so-called eccentricities.

Through severe penance and constant prayer, Philip Neri had attained great heights of holiness and contemplation. But although mystical and ecstatic, he was always at anybody's beck and call. He was the most sociable contemplative the world has ever known, for he had discovered the way of continuing to pray even when he was talking with the greatest vivacity.

Favored by God with ecstasies and visions, he tried in every way possible to prevent them. If he felt an ecstasy coming on, he would divert his attention by a joke or some humorous act. He had a great distrust of visions and rebuked people who wanted them, because he said that one can easily become puffed up with pride over them and could easily cease striving for the virtues that really constitute holiness: obedience, patience and humility. "It is dangerous to place our trust in dreams and visions," he would say, "for it is by being a good man and a good Christian that one reaches heaven." His laughter and comical antics were therefore directed toward preventing people from discovering his own union with God and God's favors to him.

But still, people knew.

Once Philip complained, "I really suffer because of what people think of me. I constantly beg God not to do anything miraculous through me which could give them the occasion to think more highly of me than they ought. And believe me, if at times anything of a supernatural character has happened, it has been through the faith of others, not through any merit on my part."

St. Philip Neri always distrusted himself. When ill, he was heard to sigh, "If I get well, I intend to change my life. Ah, poor me, how many ignorant peasants and poor girls will be far above me in heaven. Lord, beware of me today, lest I betray You. Let me get through today, and I shall not fear to-morrow."

But if Philip was stern toward himself, toward sinners he was very gentle, even whimsical.

Overcome with grief and sorrow, one man broke into uncontrollable sobs at the end of his confession. Philip let him cry and then said, "Go ahead and weep. God understands you are sorry. Didn't you ever cry on your father's shoulder? Well, let me embrace you in God's name." After some moments, St. Philip continued, "Now then, you must stop crying. You must rejoice because your sins have been forgiven. And I shall give you a special penance: You are to go to the city square and stand there and laugh for one full minute. If anyone stops to ask what you are doing, simply reply that you are rejoicing because you are a son of God."

Once a woman confessed temptations to despair. Philip answered, "Heaven is yours."

"No, Father, I am afraid I'm going to be lost."

"All right, I'll prove it to you that you won't be lost. Tell me, for whom did Christ die?"

"For sinners."

"And who or what are you?"

"A sinner."

"Well then, heaven is yours, because you are sorry for your sins."

One day, Philip was approached by a boy who had sinned so much that he did not have the courage to open up his heart.

"Come," the saint urged. "You'll feel better soon."

"Father, I've made mistakes so often...."

"They will all be forgiven you."

"Maybe, but at the cost of so much penance!"

"Nothing exceptional," Philip assured him. "Only this: every time you fall, come right back and put yourself in the state of grace."

The young man promised. He confessed himself, received absolution, and went on his way.

But he returned almost at once, head down, humiliated.

Philip Neri comforted him and encouraged him one, two, three, many, many times; always the boy returned with bowed head, weary and dejected. But then he began to return less frequently; the falls were becoming smaller and more widely separated from one another. Finally, aided by grace and virtue, the lad was well on his way to being a good Christian.

In his long life, St. Philip Neri made a great mark on the spirituality of the day and helped people acquire an easy familiarity with God.

Despite many severe illnesses, he always rallied and was active to the end.

On the evening of May 26, 1595, after a full day of hearing confessions and receiving visitors, the eighty-year-old Neri quietly rendered his happy soul to God.

20

renegade

Captain John de Lellis stomped hurriedly into the kitchen. Where *was* Camilla, anyway? he thought impatiently. There were important guests in the parlor, and they couldn't be kept waiting.

He turned sharply as he heard a shuffling sound in the next room. "Camilla, is that you?" he said aloud as he headed for the pantry. Yes, she was there, but the captain found his wife with her face in her hands, crying softly.

A servant was hastily sent to the parlor with refreshments; then the captain, half guessing the problem, asked, "It's Camillus again, isn't it?"

Camilla's grey head nodded.

"If that boy can't learn to obey," stormed the captain, "he'll have to fend for himself. No son of mine is going to share my roof and eat my food if he can't take orders!"

Camilla realized that her husband was working himself up, but her efforts to excuse the boy only added fuel to the flame.

"Quiet, woman!" the captain shouted. "We've been patient long enough. We've told him time and again, but nothing seems to stick. Now he'll learn the hard way—or not at all!"

The captain strode across the kitchen, only to meet his youngest son coming in the back door.

The exchange was short and charged to the breaking point. Broad-shouldered, six-foot Camillus, who towered over his father, gulped back his shock as the ultimatum was laid down. But quickly the cocky self-assurance and stubbornness he had allowed to grow for so long regained control. He *wouldn't* give in—never! And if that meant leaving, then he'd leave!

The weeks that followed were filled with a false sense of exhilaration, as Camillus told himself he *was* happy to be a "man" and on his own. Every whim he indulged to the full, and soon enmeshed himself in a web of gambling. This fast became an obsession with the young de Lellis. He would bet on anything and everything for the sheer thrill of adventure. However, like most people so addicted, he lost far more than he won, and was forced to replenish his funds constantly. To get money, you need a trade, Camillus reasoned. So he did what he knew how to do best—he fought. In fact, he even deigned to carry arms under his own father's command and joined the captain's troops when the Venetians asked for aid in a war with the Turks.

A small oil lamp flickered in the evening breeze. Its dancing light lent even greater sharpness to the chiseled features of two army commanders discussing the day's battle in low tones.

"You've got to admit it, de Lellis," one rumbled as he fingered his drinking mug pensively. "Whether you like it or not, your son's a real fighter—nothing can stop him in the heat of battle! Why, in size alone he's worth two of my best bowmen!"

"You're right," the captain agreed, "but the only trouble is that he doesn't stop once he's off the field. If he's not arguing with one of the officers, he's slugging one of the infantry men, or gambling away his armor at some local tavern. I'm telling you, he shrugs off discipline like it was poison. He's simply causing too much trouble among the men."

The commander was forced to agree.

"Well, now he's developed this lame foot of his," de Lellis continued. "I think it's as good an excuse as any to send him back. What do you say?"

There seemed to be no other choice, and soon Camillus was sent to Rome where he was admitted to the St. James' Hospital. For nine months the sore on his foot was nursed and cared for. At times it would seem to improve, and then it would worsen again. After a while, however, even during his convalescence, Camillus' "self-assertion" and independence earned him a none-too-friendly invitation to depart.

Groping blindly for something to fill the emptiness he was trying to ignore, Camillus returned to active duty in the Turkish war. He spent a couple more restless, quarrelsome years as a mercenary, until, in the autumn of 1574, he finally gambled away everything—his savings, his arms, his clothes— right down to the proverbial shirt, which was stripped off his back in the streets of Naples.

No better than a pauper now, Camillus no longer had the nerve to approach his father. I'll just have to find some other sort of work, he mused as he slunk through the back alleys, begging for a cast-off cloak.

It wasn't long before Camillus heard about the new Capuchin monastery going up at Manfredonia. The young man knew how to "put his shoulder to the wheel" when he had to, so he began to earn his bread there, doing construction work.

The constant sight of the monks, so serene and purposeful, men who seemed to know where they were going in life, had a gradual effect on the new laborer. In spite of himself, he was curious, and he became more and more aware of the long-suppressed vacancy in his being. He had tried so hard to fill it—but now he realized that the harder he tried, the more his attempts turned into mockeries and nightmares. There was something more, something deeper to life; he could sense it.

One afternoon, Camillus had just emptied a barrow full of stones for the masons and was on his way back for more when he nearly literally ran into Father Angelo.

"Where are you off to in such a hurry, my friend?" the monk chuckled.

This was the opening Camillus had been waiting for. He started talking, but soon he was listening as he never had listened before. This monk made sense, he thought. And he kept on thinking all the way to his lodging that night. Suddenly he was overwhelmed in a flood of grief, as he realized how he had wasted his life. And—probably for the first time in his life—he really prayed. "My God," he murmured, "it's a miracle that You have not just snuffed out my life—I'm such a repulsive creature! Twenty-five years old, and I've done nothing but offend You and run from responsibility.... My God, have mercy!" he whispered in a voice cracked with emotion.

I've got to repair somehow! This was Camillus' only thought. The next morning he hurried to the monastery far earlier than usual. Another long talk with Father Angelo, and Camillus was admitted to the novitiate of the Capuchins. "I'll make up for lost time, now," he promised his Lord as he knelt before the Blessed Sacrament.

However, the story of Camillus' life after his change of heart was far from the fairy-tale "lived happily ever after." The harnessing of his own will, long grown so domineering, was bitter medicine

for a young man who had been his own master since
his late teens. But looking back on what he had been
— or rather *hadn't* been — gave Camillus fresh courage
and renewed his determination to conquer. His powerful character was not crushed but channeled, and
aided by the grace of God, it carried him through the
expected gamut of disappointments and adjustments.

One morning, when everything seemed to be
flowing reasonably smoothly, Brother Camillus was
called to the abbot's office. The novice's brow fur-
rowed as he hurried down the corridor — that is, hurried as fast as his aching foot would allow. The
nagging sore of his fighting years had surfaced again,
and Camillus was worried that it was the subject of
the abbot's summons.

The lean, grey-haired cleric smiled kindly as
Camillus entered the room. He liked the boy and felt
certain that God had big plans for him. His smile
ended in a slight sigh though, because he did not
think those plans included Camillus' becoming a
Capuchin.

"My son," he began, "I see you're having trouble
with your foot...." The young man nodded, but tried
to stand straight and tall. He dreaded what he knew
must be coming.

"You know how strict our Rule is, don't you,
Brother?" the abbot asked. "With this disease in your
leg, you really would not be able to shoulder our life
in its entirety. We've thought a long time, Camillus,"
he continued, resting a fatherly hand on the young
man's shoulder. "You're to go to St. James' Hospital
again, and we'll see if you can be healed. While you're
there you can help in the care of the sick who are
less fortunate than yourself...."

With a heavy heart, but knowing that somehow
God would bring good out of what seemed to be the

crushing of all his dreams, Camillus set out for the familiar building in Rome.

It was a very different Camillus who arrived from the Capuchin monastery than the one who had been a patient at St. James' in previous years.

Again his illness played an ugly game of "hide-and-seek." Three separate times he was thought to be cured, and returned to the monastery—only to be sent away when the sore appeared again.

Camillus finally concluded that the life of a monk was not to be his, and he set his heart in earnest on caring for the sick at St. James'. Hospitals of his day were unbelievable by modern standards. The staff was recruited from anyone who could be induced to take on the job—sometimes even criminals worked there while serving their sentences. As a consequence, the care given the sick was often very negligent or even abusive.

Gradually, as he served all the patients he could, a plan began to take shape in Camillus' mind. He would gather together other attendants who wanted to serve out of love for God and the ideal of charity!

It was a slow, painful process, but over the years a religious order was formed. It came to be known as the Company of the Servants of the Sick. The founder, at the advice of his confessor, St. Philip Neri, studied for the priesthood and was ordained. Father Camillus then set about providing a rule for his co-workers. Charity was to be their highest goal. Each member was to consider himself as the servant, even the slave, of the patients, whom they served as if Christ Himself lay sick before them.

Wherever there was famine or plague, rampant disease or other human suffering, there the Servants of the Sick appeared, to bring both physical and spiritual comfort. They would care for the sick wherever they were to be found—in homes, in hospi-

"I assure you, as often as you did it for one of my least brothers, you did it for me."

Matthew 25:40

tals, on street corners and even on the battlefields. In 1595 and 1601 some of these religious were sent with the troops fighting in Hungary and Croatia, thus forming the first recorded "military field-ambulance corps."

Even though he carried the burdens of his own constant sickness and the direction of the rapidly expanding group, Camillus continued throughout his life to personally serve the most distasteful cases of terminal disease. It was recorded that one unfortunate man's entire face was so disfigured by a cancerous infection that no one would go near him. Camillus, however, not only served him, but even lavished extra care on him, trying to comfort the derelict in his last moments by cradling him in his arms. This incident and Camillus' whole manner were undeniable proof that his gift of self was truly total and unreserved.

Seven years after he had laid down the canonical leadership of his Order, Camillus was making a final visitation of its hospitals together with the new superior. At one point he collapsed. Sickness had sapped his strength. However, there were still more of his spiritual sons to visit for the last time, and pushing himself ahead by sheer will power, Camillus recovered enough to complete his tour. Once home again, however, he knew that he would be seeing the Lord in person very soon. On July 14, 1614, at the age of sixty-four, this one-time renegade completed his harnessing of the fire within him and presented his entire gift of self before the God he had served so long and so well.

21

God's
cinderella

In a cold, dark, musty corner of the barn stood a teenage girl peering out from one of the cracks. She had a clear view of the house. There in the twilight appeared a tall, familiar figure.

"It's father!" Germaine said half aloud.

Laurent Cousin strolled slowly up to the house. Mrs. Cousin had been anxiously awaiting his return, and she was a woman who didn't like to be kept waiting. When he opened the door he was greeted with, "Don't just stand there. Come in and close that door. You're late. What kept you?"

Germaine winced as she heard that rasping voice. She watched the door shut, then sauntered over to another spot in the barn that she called her bedroom. There on some straw she sank to the ground. One of the lambs wandered over next to her.

"You're so soft and silent, little one," the girl whispered as she caressed it.

The lambs were just about the only visible things she had to talk to. However, she often spoke with God, the Blessed Mother, and her guardian angel. They were her closest friends.

Meanwhile, inside the house, Mr. Cousin was taking off his hat.

"Old man George was behind in getting the hay into the barn," he said.

"I've already heard that excuse four times this week." Madame Cousin shook her head and stirred the soup faster.

Happy to see their father, the children were already vying with one another, trying to be the first to greet him. After they had displayed all their exuberance in hugs and kisses, the family settled down to eat.

"Did anyone bring Germaine supper?" Laurent asked his wife.

"No. And no one will until after we have eaten. Come on now, before everything gets cold."

Laurent swallowed hard to get his soup down. Nothing hurt him more than his wife's attitude toward Germaine. He couldn't understand it.

Immediately after the meal he got up, took what food he could and went straight to the barn.

"Germaine! Germaine!" he called.

"Father!" Germaine ran as fast as she could. "How are you, Father?"

"Fine! I brought your supper." Germaine and her father sat down together on a low pile of bundled hay.

"Mother makes delicious bread," said the girl. "I wish I could learn and be of some help. Sometimes she looks so tired. Today I offered to carry a bucket of feed down to the chicken coop. After I promised to be careful and not lose anything from the bucket, she let me take it."

"Very good, Germaine. Your stepmother does have a lot to do, and I'm sure she appreciates your help. Say! What's that black-and-blue mark on your arm?"

"Well, Father, it took a while to feed those chickens and so the sheep were late getting to pasture. Stepmother was pretty upset and punished me for being so lazy."

"Oh.... Well, you get a good night's rest." Laurent leaned over and kissed Germaine on the forehead. "Good night," he said.

"Good night, Father."

As he walked back to the house, his heart ached. It pained him to think of his wife's cruelty. Couldn't she see the girl's good will? What did she expect? So many thoughts ran through his mind. When he reached the house Laurent sighed heavily. Poor Germaine, so deformed and sick, yet so virtuous and good! To her stepmother she was nothing but a sick, ugly cripple who had to be kept away from the rest of the family. But even though Germaine was ugly to look at, wasn't she also a child who had feelings like other children of her age? What she needed was a little love and care.

"Germaine, today I want you to take the sheep to the edge of the Bouconne forest. If anything happens to those sheep, girl, you'd better not come home."

"Bouconne forest?" Germaine exclaimed in surprise.

"You heard what I said. And I'm warning you again, don't let anything happen to those sheep."

"Yes, Mother."

The Bouconne forest was noted for the packs of hungry wolves that roamed there. Lately there had even been reports of them venturing out of the forest in search of food. All the farm folk were so frightened that they avoided the section as much as possible. What was Madame Cousin trying to prove?

Germaine did as her stepmother ordered. The forest provided plenty of good grazing — there was no doubt about that. But there was no doubt about the starving wolves either. Germaine could occasionally hear the rustling of leaves and growls, but she calmly prayed that God would protect her and the sheep.

Madame Cousin made sure she was there that night when Germaine came home. Surprised to see her stepmother waiting for her, Germaine waved as she approached the barn, but Madame Cousin did not return the greeting. As soon as Germaine came up to her, she asked roughly.

"Did you bring back all the sheep?"

"Yes, stepmother," Germaine said smiling.

"Are you sure? Did you count them? You're not lying to me, are you?"

"Lying! Oh no! All the sheep are safe."

"I guess you know what's good for you. Tomorrow you'll go back there again," Madame Cousin said coldly.

The following day Germaine again pastured the sheep at the edge of the Bouconne forest. The beautiful, sunny day passed peacefully, and Germaine was busily spinning the wool her stepmother had given her when suddenly from behind she heard the rustling of leaves. She turned quickly. There, coming up the forest path, was a poor beggar.

"Sorry if I startled you," the man called.

"Oh! Oh, you didn't startle me," stammered Germaine. "Come over here and sit down. You look tired."

"I haven't eaten since yesterday morning. Do you have some food you could give to a poor, old man like me?"

Germaine reached into her sack and pulled out a few crusts of bread. "You are welcome to what I have," she said as she offered them to him.

Gratefully the man reached for the crusts. "Thank you, little girl. You'll never know how much I appreciate this. I was beginning to wonder if I was going to end up as food for those starving wolves. You know, this isn't a very safe place for you to be. Once they get wind of the sheep, I'm afraid there won't be much left."

"Oh, don't worry about the wolves. I don't think they like us being here, but they won't do anything about it," Germaine jokingly replied.

Germaine's new friend wasn't laughing. He was concerned for her and the flock.

"I'm telling you, they'll attack as soon as they feel sure of themselves."

"I have to go now," Germaine said, "but tomorrow I'll bring you more food."

As the sun began to set on another day, Germaine hurriedly gathered the sheep and headed home. She seldom ate all the bread she was given. Each day she would make a little sacrifice and put some aside for any poor beggar that might pass by. That particular evening Germaine went to get her "savings." She dug deep into the hay. It was gone! Everything was gone! While the girl had been at the Bouconne forest that day, Madame Cousin had taken the few pieces of bread Germaine had put aside.

The girl's first thought was, "My poor beggar! What shall I give him?"

Taking all her courage, Germaine headed straight for the kitchen door. She tiptoed in and closed the door softly. Her eyes immediately fell on a jar. Picking up the cover, she found the missing bread, and some straw still stuck to it. Germaine shook the contents of the jar into her apron and started to leave.

"What are you doing in this house, you dirty little girl?" Madame Cousin burst into the room. "Steal my bread to give to those good-for-nothings will you?"

Madame Cousin was furious. She grabbed a large wooden stick and threatened to beat Germaine. The girl pulled her apron tightly to herself and ran. Her stepmother shouted: "Thief! Thief!"

All the neighbors flocked out to see what was going on. They had never known Madame Cousin to be so upset. She was actually running after Germaine with that club.

"If she catches up with her, she'll kill that poor girl," yelled one of the men.

Germaine's heart pounded inside her. She was gasping for air. Her legs just wouldn't move any more.

One of the neighbor women tried to hold Madame Cousin back, but she was so excited that there wasn't any reasoning with her. "Stop! Stop!" the woman gasped. "Don't hit her!"

Madame Cousin raised her stick and commanded, "Let down that apron and show everyone what a thief you are!"

Germaine dropped the hem of her apron, and there in front of everyone fell the most beautiful assortment of spring flowers.

Shocked, bewildered and a bit embarrassed, Madame Cousin quietly told Germaine to go back to the barn.

Besides the miracle of the flowers, another miracle seemed to have taken place — a conversion in the heart of Madame Cousin. At least she was no longer as harsh and downright cruel as she had been. There were never really any formal apologies or informal ones for that matter, but there *were* some notable changes.

However, as someone put it, the eleventh hour had come for Germaine. One morning in the summer of 1601, Germaine was found dead on her bed of straw.

Her life had consisted of twenty-two years of sickness, beatings, loneliness and lack of love.

Although Germaine has passed to her reward, the memory of her lives on as an heroic and encouraging example for us all.

On June 29, 1867, Pope Pius IX officially proclaimed her Saint Germaine.

22

gentle
shepherd

It was something like looking into a kaleidoscope. A dizzy maze of bright colors swirled through the streets. Music, song, laughter and hand clapping strove to outdo one another. The very air vibrated at the highest pitch of excitement.

It was the year 1602. Annecy's holy and zealous priest, Francis de Sales, had just been consecrated Bishop of Geneva.

The people of France, where the bishop was to reside, had known Francis de Sales ever since he was a child. They had watched him grow, and some had even attended his ordination. The people trusted him; when in trouble they had always sought him out. And when they had been unable to come to Father Francis, *he* had gone to them. There was no doubt in anyone's mind that Geneva would have a fine bishop.

That first winter as bishop, Francis was anxious and disturbed. Religious ignorance was widespread. He could see so many public sins being committed. "Forgive them, Father," he silently prayed, "for they don't know what they are doing." One Sunday, after much prayer and sacrifice, the bishop addressed his flock.

"My dear people, I, your bishop, wish to begin teaching classes on our holy Faith. I would encourage you all—men, women and children, young and old—to attend. These classes will be held every Sunday afternoon at one o'clock, here at the church. May almighty God bless you, in the name of the Father, and of the Son and of the Holy Spirit."

After Mass was over, the bishop was pleased to see the people's interest and enthusiasm.

"I'll be there, Your Excellency," said an elderly woman, "and so will my husband."

The bishop smiled. Then he caught sight of a boy he recognized as one of the mischief-makers of the town.

"And what about you?" Francis asked as he put his hand on the boy's shoulder. "Will you come to my classes, too?"

"Sure. Why not?" came the sheepish reply.

Some came out of admiration, others purely out of curiosity and others out of a love for the novel. Whatever their reasons, the church was packed. And it was packed the next week, too, and the next....

Bishop de Sales' fame spread. One of the neighboring dioceses invited him to preach the Lenten sermons in a town called Dijon.

Francis was undecided.

"There is a lot of work to be done right here in Annecy. I pray that God will not reprove me for leaving my flock to go and preach to someone else's in Dijon."

But it was God who was calling de Sales to Dijon. Some urgent business turned up and the bishop was forced to accept the invitation to preach.

Again, the name "Bishop of Geneva" drew enormous crowds. People felt that there was something "special" either about him or about what he said. When he spoke, all his attention was focused on the crowd, and they knew that he was speaking to each of them.

After preaching several times, Francis noticed the unusual attention of a particular young woman.

One day, after delivering his customary sermon, he stood talking with the Archbishop of Bourges as the people filed out of the church.

"That young woman dressed in black..." whispered de Sales, "who is she?"

"The one who is greeting us now is my sister, Baroness de Chantal. She is a widow and has asked to meet you," the archbishop replied.

"It would be my pleasure. Tell her the Bishop of Geneva wishes to speak to her."

Thus took place the first meeting of two future saints — Francis de Sales and Jane Frances de Chantal.

During one of their first visits, Madame de Chantal (a woman in every sense of the word) made it a point to dress in her very best. After all, it wasn't very often that the Bishop of Geneva visited Dijon. Nor was it very often that Madame de Chantal had the honor of being in the presence of such a famous person.

Austere in his own dress, however, the bishop remarked, "What are your plans for the future now that you are a widow? You're a lovely woman, madame. I would imagine you must be thinking of remarrying?"

"Absolutely not, Your Excellency!" she exclaimed.

"Well, then," smiled the bishop, "may I dare say that without those jewels you would look just as lovely."

Without a word Madame de Chantal removed her precious necklace and pins. She never wore them again.

That was what everyone loved about Bishop Francis—he was holy and gracious, but to the point!

While on one of his long and tiresome journeys, Francis fell sick and was forced to take to bed. As he lay there exhausted and in pain, he happened to overhear some heckling in the adjoining room.

"I guess our fat saint isn't accustomed to so much traveling. You'd never imagine it from the size of him."

"Tom," called the bishop to one of his companions, "find out who that is and invite him in to see me."

The young heckler was not too eager to accept the invitation, especially so soon after criticizing the bishop.

When Francis found out that this young man was the son of a doctor, he began to describe his illness.

"What would you suggest?" he asked. "I'm sure you have some knowledge of medicine."

The lad swallowed hard in an effort to rid himself of his pride and embarrassment. "Well...well...," he stammered.

Well, as far as Francis was concerned, "the operation was a success." In the course of the conversation, the young man was soon revealing all his doubts and objections regarding the Faith and listening attentively to every word the bishop spoke. As the hours passed, their friendship grew. Toward evening the bishop asked the youth if he would like to be his traveling companion. The young man was practically speechless.

"This way we can talk some more about religion," the bishop said, smiling.

At the end of their journey the young man asked to become a Catholic, and needless to add, the bishop never had a more devoted friend from that day forward.

Francis had a heart for others. He could almost sense the needs of people simply by speaking a few words with them. The lines outside his confessional box were always long. Stories began to circulate that one did not even have to state his sins; this priest knew them already.

One day a man went to confession to Francis and began listing his sins. His confession was hurried and apparently without much sorrow.

After listening a few moments, Francis could no longer control himself and let a loud sob escape him. The man kneeling there stared through the grate. "Are you okay?" he asked. "Is there something I can do?"

"Be sorry for your sins," came the reply. "I am weeping because of your complacency. Be truly sorry and weep for your sins."

The man was so shocked and ashamed that he performed the penance Francis gave him and changed his way of living.

In an effort to keep his flock strong in the Faith, Francis wrote his *Introduction to the Devout Life*. Later he wrote the *Treatise on the Devout Life* for those seeking greater devotion.

And in 1610, with Madame de Chantal, he founded the Visitation Order. This was just twelve years before his death.

In autumn, 1622, the bishop was asked when he would like to see the tailors about his winter trousseau.

"There won't be any need to call them. I'm sure they will be happy at the thought of all the material they will be saving," he jokingly remarked. That very autumn the bishop's health took a turn for the worse. It was apparent that the Divine Master was calling His faithful servant. Although pain, nausea and exhaustion drained him of every ounce of energy, this holy prelate never once complained or showed himself irritable.

If the Bishop of Geneva had drawn crowds before, he was now drawing masses. People were constantly seeking his prayers, advice or simply a look at him.

One day he was sitting just inside the open door of one of the convents of the Visitation. Outside, the usual crowd had gathered, each one anxious to catch a glimpse of the holy bishop.

"Sitting in that draft isn't good for you, Your Excellency. Why don't you close the door?" asked one of the sisters from behind the grille.

Obedient as always, Francis got up and shuffled to the door. The sisters watched as he paused for a moment in the doorway. There before him stood a mixture of people he knew and loved...people who knew and loved him.

Moved almost to the point of tears, Francis fell back into his chair.

"How can I close the door on these children?" he exclaimed.

Shortly afterwards, at eight o'clock in the evening of December 28, 1622, the door of this life was shut for Francis de Sales. Forty-three years later, the gentle shepherd was acclaimed a saint of the Church.

23

woman
of
proven
worth

"But, sir! You've *got* to believe that Jesus Christ is present in the Blessed Sacrament...."

A surprised silence, broken only by the crackling of a large fire on the hearth, followed five-year-old Jane's emphatic statement. Her father looked on, rather nonplused, as she continued to set forth her line of reasoning to their Huguenot visitor.

"You *have* to believe it, because Jesus Himself said so!"

Chuckling a little, though he was impressed in spite of himself at her earnestness, the nobleman reached for a dish of sugared almonds on the table.

"Come now, Jane," he chided sweetly. "I think you'll be far more interested in these than in our theological discussion."

Jane curtsied politely and held out her tiny, frilled apron to receive the gift. But she was a lawyer's daughter and would not be put off by niceties. Promptly she tumbled the entire contents into the open fireplace and continued determinedly.

14. *Moments of Decision*

"This," she said as the last almond hit the flames, "is what happens to people who don't believe what our Lord says."

Despite her bombastic approach, the guest was not offended and during his stay Jane spoke to him often with her startling frankness. She truly was her father's daughter.

Jeanne-Françoise Frémyot was born in Dijon, France, on January 23, 1572. Her mother died before she was two years old and Jane and her brother and sister were brought up by her father with the occasional help of an aunt.

Monsieur Frémyot was an upright man of absolute integrity, clear-sighted, brave, just and interested in his children. He had regular discussion sessions with them on religion, history and the humanities—in much the same way that, earlier in the century, a lawyer on the Thames in Chelsea, England, Sir Thomas More, had instructed his own children. Jane learned much more from her father than mere academic knowledge—he structured her character upon a strong, bold framework. She would be compelled to rely on this very much in her life.

The Bourbilly castle lay in thickly forested lands in the vicinity of Dijon. December of 1592 saw it smothered cosily under a blanket of midwinter snows; an abundance of richly decorated sleighs and garlands at the entrances signaled festivities of some magnitude. The chapel especially blazed with color and excitement and was filled to capacity. At the altar knelt a young couple, heads bowed as they received the blessing of their marriage vows; Baron de Chantal soon led his young bride down the aisle and the two mingled happily with the numerous guests in the great hall of the castle. Jane, now Madame de Chantal and Baroness of the Bourbilly estate, was sure she must be floating at least six inches off the ground! Her joy knew no bounds as her eyes met those of Christopher and their gaze locked. Words were not needed to communicate what they felt and shared.

Winter melted swiftly into spring and each passing day drew the young couple ever closer. They shared many common interests, Jane discovered, for Christopher was an avid reader and well-versed in many of the topics which she had so loved to discuss with her father. In the early evening they would often walk together up and down the wide avenue leading to the castle deep in conversation and oblivious to all else. Theirs had been a fairy-tale wedding and it looked as if their peace and mutual happiness could never be disturbed.

But with the return of spring there was a resumption of fighting in the turbulent France of the time. Baron de Chantal, along with his men-at-arms, was expected to join the king in his campaign. Christopher thought long and hard about how he would break the news to his wife—not only did he have to leave, but *she* would be left with the immense task of managing the estate, and she was barely twenty-one. Finally the young baron simply blurted out the whole situation one evening as they were taking one of their customary walks:

"Jane," he began, "I have to go away...."

He heard her draw her breath in sharply.

"I was half expecting it," she murmured softly. "There are rumors all over that the war is starting up again...."

"I think it will be like this for quite some time, too," he continued. "Oh, I don't mean that I won't be home at all, but it *will* mean almost constant coming and going. It's my duty, Jane," he said firmly, answering the unspoken pleading in her eyes.

Then he began to explain the present state of Bourbilly. His father had always preferred fighting to farming, and as a result had left all his domestic affairs in the hands of his capable wife, who had managed them well until her death, ten years before.

"And now things just aren't as they should be," the baron continued. "Our lands are still fruitful and in good condition, but the stewards and farmers are in the habit of running things pretty much as they please. There's a good deal of reorganizing to be done and I've tried to get it started these past few months—but now it will be in your hands, Jane."

Jane's neatly bonnetted head swung around quickly, and she stopped in the middle of the path to confront her husband. "I can't" was written all over her face.

"But listen, my dear," he pleaded quietly. "I know you can do it. Look at my mother—she was even less prepared than you are for country life, since she was raised in court at Paris, yet she learned. And she kept on, even when she was so ill. For years before her death she was wracked with pain from morning to night, but she carried the full load until God took her. I can remember her saying once, 'We must face each day with courage, Christopher. God will compensate for our deficiencies and record eternally every effort we make in His name to do our duty.'"

Jane could see by the light in his eyes just how much he thought of his mother. Her example did impress Jane deeply. Slowly the knot of resistance melted and the young baroness resolved not only to shoulder the burden but to put every ounce of her strength and talent into doing a good job.

Though Madame de Chantal was especially gifted for organization and management, she had never cared for it, and always found the position distasteful; but this type of burden would never really be lifted from her throughout her lifetime, since it would be one of her most time-consuming obligations even later, when she would be a foundress. Like it or not, however, she would do what she was called upon to do now by her husband, and later by God.

The estate was soon humming along smoothly again, as Jane tackled the huge task of giving a framework and form to life there. A resident chaplain was called in so that each day could begin with Mass for all in the household; servants were given specific charges and strict account was kept of fields and crops. She added new emphasis to one dimension which soon became her trademark, so to speak, throughout the district, and this was her constant, open-handed charity. Of course, almsgiving was something expected of the nobility, but Madame de Chantal was different. She put her *self* into her giving. In time of famine, she had an outdoor stove and oven built, just so there would be a constant supply of hot soup and bread for the poor, whom she served with her own hands. The sick in all the surrounding villages knew her compassion firsthand. She would visit frequently, riding on horseback to the homes of the most needy; no disease was too revolting for her to give her care; she seemed to be everywhere at once, with a ready smile, a cheerful word and even competent medicinal help. She had a particular love for young mothers; quietly, simply she helped them in childbirth and the critical days following.

It was related by a contemporary of hers that the baroness had been at the bedside of one such mother all day, but had had to leave before the child was born. Later on in the evening, when mother and baby were resting peacefully, the husband glanced out his front door by chance. He was taken aback to see Madame de Chantal on her knees near his threshold. She had returned to pray for his wife's safe delivery and to be on hand if she were needed. Indeed, Jane Frances gave of herself as well as her goods.

For nine years life at Bourbilly continued peacefully; Christopher came home at every opportunity, and the couple's love and understanding of each other were evident to all who knew them. The family grew gradually; though Jane's first two children died soon after birth, by 1601 there were three young faces at the Chantal table, and a fourth cooing happily in a nearby crib.

About this time the baron decided to retire from active court duty, both over a matter of conscience—something he had been ordered to do which he did not feel was just—and also because of his health (he had contracted dysentery in one of the campaigns). Patiently and lovingly Jane nursed him back to his full vigor. By early autumn he was impatient to be up and about again.

Two weeks after Charlotte, their last child, was born, a cousin and good friend of the baron stopped at the castle to offer his congratulations for Christopher's recovery and the youngest daughter's birth. The two men were soon avidly discussing the latest hunting techniques and the best places for finding game. Monsieur d'Anlezy suddenly suggested an afternoon of deer-stalking, to which Christopher eagerly agreed.

Not even two hours after they had so happily left, a dazed servant half ran, half stumbled up the path to the castle.

"Call Madame de Chantal," he panted, "right away! The baron has been wounded; he's in the

"When one finds a worthy wife,
  her value is far beyond pearls.
She reaches out her hands to the poor,
  and extends her arms to the needy.
Give her a reward of her labors,
  and let her works praise her at the
    city gates."

Proverbs 31:10, 20, 31

cottage by the mill; he said not to worry...nothing serious...but...."

The maid barely heard the last words as she flew out of the kitchen and up the stairs; the baroness was resting—in fact she had not really been on her feet much at all since Charlotte's birth—but she was up before the maid could even help her, racing to her husband's side.

Nine days of tense agony followed. Christopher knew he would not make it and was resigned to the fact. But every time he spoke of death Jane would change the subject quickly, for she would not hear of it. Her prayers were continuous and almost fierce as she begged, entreated, even demanded that God spare her husband. At one point she slipped from Christopher's room and ran alone into the woods, crying her prayer aloud:

"Take all I have, my children, everything, but leave me my husband!" However, God was to answer her in another way. Christopher turned his thoughts to eternity, received the last sacraments and died peacefully just a little over a week after the accident. Then and only then did Jane say her "yes"; it did not lessen her grief, but it did serve as a bridge drawing her gradually closer to God, as she struggled to accept His will.

Months of mourning followed, during which Madame de Chantal strove to smile bravely as guests came to offer sympathy and comfort. Then she received a letter from her father-in-law summoning her and her children to his manor in Monthelon. "I am old now," he wrote, "and I do not yet know my grandchildren...," whom he threatened to disinherit if she did not come. This was simply his way, the baroness understood that. But she hesitated, since she knew the man had given up his faith and was not living a good life. In the end, hoping to do him good, she accepted.

During the seven and a half years that followed, Jane was treated little better than a servant. A loose-living woman, a sort of head servant, ran the house *and* the baron. Madame de Chantal was barely tolerated and made to ask permission for every detail. Everything natural within her rebelled, but she swallowed down resentment and ill will, repaid the servant with her generous kindness, and continued to carry out all the charity she possibly could. She set up a small school for the children in the area, and a dispensary for the sick, both of which she staffed herself.

It was during her second Lent there at Monthelon that she received another letter, one which would change her life and give direction to her wandering, searching spirit. The Bishop of Geneva was preaching in Dijon, and her brother had invited her to come to hear him. Daily she attended Francis de Sales' sermons and the result is well known: under his counseling she came to see that God wanted her total donation—and she gave unhesitatingly. Everywhere she met with strong opposition and scorn—the young baroness had everything to live for...why should she become a nun? But within a few years of her first meeting with Francis, Jane saw to it that her children were properly settled and consecrated herself completely to God and His will. Gradually a new religious Order formed around her, the Visitation Sisters, whose apostolate was to be an outgrowth of her own charitable works: teaching and caring for the sick poor.

Nothing was ever easy, but Mérè de Chantal placed her trust in God unreservedly. After serving

Him and the community for nearly forty years of intense prayer and exhausting activity, she passed into eternity on December 13, 1641, after a prolonged agony.

Her deep, practical spirituality is a legacy even today, and the words of Proverbs come spontaneously to mind:

"...her value is far beyond pearls....
'Many are the women of proven worth,
    but you have excelled them all.'
Charm is deceptive and beauty fleeting;
    the woman who fears the Lord is to be praised.
Give her a reward of her labors...."

                                              (Prv. 31:10, 29-30)

24

a
man
among
men

It was November 3, 1639 — a day from all appearances just like any other. In Lima, Peru, however, it was not an ordinary day. It was a day of tragedy and of triumph — of tragedy because Peru had lost one of her best-loved sons, of triumph, because this son was Lima's glory.

In a small room of the Dominican monastery of the Holy Rosary, the commanding voice of the Archbishop of Mexico City suddenly broke through the stillness:

"Let us all learn from the edifying death of Brother Martin how to die well. It is a lesson which is most important and most difficult."

Martin de Porres' body was laid out before the main altar in the monastery chapel. Then the doors of the chapel were thrown open to permit Martin's closest friends — the poor, the homeless, the old and the sick — to bid him a final farewell.

The bright sunlight filtered through the stained-glass windows. Martin's black skin and sharp features stood out magnificently against his white Dominican habit.

As the body grew colder and more rigid, a disappointed confrere, who had hoped for a miracle that would indicate Martin's holiness, went near and chided affectionately, "Why is your body stiff and rigid, Brother Martin? Ask God to show His almighty power by permitting it to remain lifelike." Such faith did not go unrewarded. Within a few moments, a fragrance of roses and lilies issued from the coffin and Martin's rigid body relaxed and grew soft.

Now there was no way to hold back the crowds. The people cut Brother Martin's habit to shreds, and it had to be replaced several times. Numerous authenticated miracles took place.

All was glory for Martin now, but it had not always been so....

Martin's story had begun just sixty years earlier.

He was the son of an African slave girl and a Spanish nobleman who deserted her shortly after the birth of Martin's younger sister, Juana. Unlike other children, Martin learned at a very early age just how bitter life can be.

"Half-breed"—he heard people whisper in undertones as he passed through the more fashionable quarters of Lima on his way back home to Espiritu Santo, the poorest section of the city. But Martin's bright face never clouded, and his happy disposition never changed. He smiled and waved to passers-by as he skipped to and fro through busy city streets. Martin's job as a delivery boy added a few coins to his mother's meager earnings. By the time he was eight, he had learned where he could buy the most for the least amount of money.

Shopkeepers and open-air merchants kept their eyes peeled so as not to miss his daily visit. They knew that the food Martin bought at the market was not all for himself, nor only for his mother and sister. In fact, he gave away more than half of it to his beggar

friends, who hemmed him in on all sides. But frequently it happened that Martin gave away more than
half; he gave away everything he had. Then he would
turn to old Tomas. As Martin told him his hard-luck
story, old Tomas would laughingly refill Martin's
basket and send him on his way with a warning,
"Remember, go straight home this time."

But one day old Tomas stopped and eyed Martin
strangely. "Do you know who is on the ship that
docked this morning?"

Now that's a strange question, Martin thought.
"Sailors, I guess," he replied.

"No Martin, not just sailors. Your father, Don
Juan de Porres, is on that boat."

"Don Juan—my father—is in Lima *now*?"
Martin was so excited that he nearly dropped his
basket.

"But there's nothing to eat in the house and it's
all my fault. I gave everything away."

Tomas suppressed a laugh, cleared his throat
and tried to appear serious. "Yes, we'll have to take
care of that. Here you go..." and he began filling the
basket.

There was a pause, and then a meek voice asked,
"Tomas? ...May I have one ripe mango for my little
sister and a piece of that nice loaf of bread over
there on the shelf for my mother?"

The old man took a few mangoes and the whole
loaf of bread from the shelf and put everything in
Martin's basket, purposely turning his back so the
boy would not see the tears in his eyes.

That boy's heart is bigger than all Peru, Tomas
was thinking. He's always worrying about someone
else, never himself.

First Martin skipped, then trotted and then
raced toward home. He ran so fast that his neighbors
in Espiritu Santo looked to see who was chasing him.

He pounded on the unlocked door. It was opened by Juana, who eyed him quizzically. Martin dashed inside, dropped his basket on the table and gave a quick glance around the poor house. He caught his breath, and then, with a manner and tone of voice far beyond his age, he announced seriously, "Juana, our father is here in Lima and he is coming to see us."

"Our father?" wide-eyed Juana responded. "Do you mean we have a father, too?"

"Yes, and we'll have to tidy up the house and put on our church clothes...."

In the space of a few weeks, great changes took place in Martin's life. He and Juana went to Ecuador, where they lived with their father's uncle, Don Diego. Well accustomed to lacking even the barest necessities, the children were overwhelmed by the lifestyle of their wealthy relatives.

Martin remained in Ecuador almost three years, but he never forgot his poor mother, whom he had left behind in Lima. Although the boy was grateful for all that his father and Don Diego were doing for him, his heart ached when he thought of how lonely his mother must be.

He began his return journey to Lima with an air of expectancy. Not only would he see his mother again, but he would be an apprentice to a surgeon. Once he learned the profession, he would be able to give genuine help to his friends, the beggars in the market place of Lima.

Martin found his mother living in surroundings vastly different from those in which he had left her. She had beautiful furniture and her house had tiled and marbled floors. There was food in abundance.

By the time Martin was twelve, he had been apprenticed to Doctor de Rivero. The youth took up a heavy round of prayer, work, study and visits to the sick. Whatever money he made was spent on the poor, and once again he became a regular visitor to the market place, where he gave out food to his long-time friends.

A year or two after Martin went to study with Doctor de Rivero, the Señora de Luna, keeper of the house where the boy was staying, was abruptly awakened early one morning by a loud noise in the street. As she passed Martin's room, she noticed a sliver of light under the door.

"He must have fallen asleep studying," she said to herself. "I'd better wake him up and make him go to bed."

The landlady knocked on the door, but there was no answer. She tried a second time. Still no answer. Then the door swung open. The Señora de Luna gasped in astonishment. Wrapt in a state of ecstasy, Martin was kneeling in front of a crucifix, his whole body enveloped in a bright light. She closed the door again and thanked God for having given her the privilege of lodging a person so dear to Him.

Now more and more, one could hear talk in the streets of people who had been helped by Martin in strange and almost miraculous ways.

Another year passed and Martin longed to do something more for God. After praying for light and guidance, he presented himself to the prior of the Dominican Monastery of the Holy Rosary. He told the priest that he would like to live at the monastery as a lay helper.

A few days later, fifteen-year-old Martin said goodbye to all his friends, packed up his medical instruments and left for the Dominican monastery. Shortly after his arrival, he was assigned to work in the monastery hospital, where he accomplished wonders for souls as well as bodies. Then, at the express wish of the superiors, Martin made his novitiate and became a professed Dominican brother.

The amount of work he continued to do was miraculous in itself. But even more miraculous were the countless and inexplicable cures he obtained.

For thirty-six years after his profession, Martin labored hard and long, with never a complaint or a moment of respite. His holiness was so overpowering that even dumb animals obeyed him.

At the end of October, 1639, Brother Martin suddenly fell ill. Although death did not seem imminent, he himself predicted that the end was near. The first days of November saw a sudden turn for the worse. Because of his high fever, one of the priests suggested that he invoke the help of St. Dominic.

"Oh," replied Martin, "I am very happy because I do not have to call on our holy Father. I have already had him here, in the company of the Mother of God, St. Joseph and St. Vincent Ferrer, the great preacher and wonder-worker of our glorious Order."

Soon after this, Martin asked for a crucifix. For several hours he was lost in deep contemplation of the Savior's sufferings. In the meantime, all the members of the community gathered around his bedside. Martin begged them to forgive him for any "bad example" he might have given. Then he took final leave of his brothers. He smiled, pressed the crucifix to his heart and rendered his soul to his Creator.

Martin had been a man among men, big enough to dominate the prejudice some might have felt regarding his racial origin. He must be admired not only for his achievements in the sphere of Christian charity but also for his personal conviction that the roots of charity lie deep in the soul, having been placed there by God, in whose image are made all men, whatever color their skin may be.

25

these
are
my
brothers

Cautiously, twelve canoes pushed their way up the St. Lawrence River. The August sun defiantly raised its flaming head above the trees to glare down on the party of eighteen Hurons and five Frenchmen kneeling in the canoes, paddling smoothly. One of the Frenchmen, thirty-six-year-old Father Isaac Jogues, sat on his haunches in the lead boat. He had been working as a missionary among the Hurons for the past six years. Active and eagle-eyed, he was well liked by the natives. They accepted a white man if he knew how to walk long miles, carry heavy burdens and eat vermin-infected food without complaint. And Father Jogues, with his broad smile, knew how to do all this and more.

Chief Eustace, the head of the expedition and Father Jogues' most promising convert, suddenly signaled the others to follow him toward shore. His sharp eyes had spotted canoe markings on the sands which he wanted to investigate. The danger of an ambush from the hostile Iroquois was a constant threat. Pointing a bronzed finger at the markings and moccasined footprints, Eustace grunted, "Iroquois! But no more than three canoes. Let us go on."

After Father Jogues had led his Huron converts in prayer, they boarded their canoes again and slipped cautiously through inshore reeds until they reached open waters. They then stroked on into the main channel, where they strung out into single file for safety's sake. When they reached a weedy, open swampland, everyone sighed in relief.

Suddenly, war whoops rent the air. The swamp-weeds came alive with red-painted bodies. Eustace and his men shrieked defiance and drove their canoes fiercely toward the enemy. Another blood-curdling shriek—this time from the river! Eustace whirled. There, bearing down upon them were eight canoes of screaming Iroquois! The Hurons had been surrounded completely. Soon the Indians were fighting hand-to-hand—about five Iroquois to each Huron.

During the struggle, Father Jogues managed to hide himself amid the tall reeds. "If I crept through the weeds to that thicket on the right," he mused, "I could steal through the forest and escape down-river. The Iroquois are too busy...." But what of his French comrades and his Huron Christians? And what about the other Hurons—those not yet baptized—who had also been captured? "The idea of flight appalled me," Father Jogues was later to write. "Could I desert my poor savages without giving them the aid which the Church of my God had entrusted to me?"

Father Jogues rose to his feet, and picked his way through the weeds toward the Iroquois, who were binding their prisoners. The braves stared at the priest in amazement. They crouched tensely, prepared for some kind of attack.

"Don't be afraid!" the Blackrobe shouted. He stretched out his arms as a sign of surrender.

Several Iroquois braves approached slowly and cautiously, then leaped upon the priest, knocked him to the ground, beat him, kicked him, and tore off the black robe. They dragged him to the other prisoners, who now numbered twenty-three. The Mohawks tortured their captives horribly and then threw them into canoes and shoved off.

That night, on a hilltop south of the St. Lawrence, Father Jogues wept over his loss. He grieved not because he and his comrades would have sufferings to offer to God, but because almost no leaders remained among the Huron Christians. These men who had been captured were the cream of the crop; they were to have been apostles among their brethren. Now they would suffer and die for their Faith—but they would never preach it. In the blackness, one comforting thought came to the missionary: "The blood of martyrs has ever been the seed of the Church." Yet he could not help but weep.

Rivers, rapids and lakes vanished behind the travelers as they made their way southward into the land of the Mohawk Iroquois. On the eighth day after the ambush, the travelers met a band of two hundred Iroquois camped on an island in Lake Champlain. These greeted the raiding party with shrieks of glee, for they were eager to honor their pagan war gods by torturing the captives. They sprang upon the Frenchmen and Hurons, beating and pounding them. Then the prisoners were made to run the "gauntlet." All the native warriors formed two lines. Each had a club or thorny rod with which he struck the prisoners as they ran between them. Father Jogues was kept until the last.

He stepped forward, tensed, and began to run up the hill between the lines of savage, swinging clubs. It was an ocean of pain—stabbing pain, dull pain, pain that sent his head reeling and spinning. Someone tripped him; he stumbled to his feet and ran on blindly, only to feel his path blocked by another mocking savage, and another and another. And all the time the clubs buffeted him, amid frenzied screams and wild, mocking laughter. He broke away again and again and stumbled on...and finally fell heavily. Blows and kicks rained upon him, but he knew no more.

When Father Jogues came to, he found himself near a platform on the hilltop. There he suffered more torture. In fact, he and his companions met with the same treatment in village after village of the fierce Iroquois.

Finally, Father Isaac and a companion, René Goupil, were taken as slaves by one of the chiefs. The two Frenchmen were so weak that they could not work; they could barely drag themselves from place to place. Pus oozed from their unhealed wounds, and clouds of fleas, lice and bugs swarmed about them. With their maimed and mangled hands, chopped and crushed by Indian cruelty, the prisoners could not ward off the insects. To add to their misery, they were half-starved, and since food was scarce among the Indians, they were given only a little ground corn and some raw squash each day. At last the Mohawks realized how sick their prisoners were, and gave them a few little fish and some pieces of meat, that they might regain their strength. As soon as the captives could hobble about again, they were sent into the fields with the squaws to harvest corn and vegetables. So the months dragged on.

"If I am to live among these people, I must try to find a way to teach them about God," Father Jogues resolved. He busied himself in learning the language well, finding ways to slip in a word here and there about the Creator of all men. After all, were not these Mohawks his brothers, bought by the blood of Christ?

"The Lord is my light and my salvation
   whom should I fear?
The Lord is my life's refuge;
   of whom should I be afraid?"

Psalm 27:1

Father Jogues also acted as his master's official beast of burden, paddling the chief's canoe down the rivers south of the Catskill mountains as his master and other chiefs went about collecting tribute from the Susquehannock Indians. The journeys gave Father Jogues a chance to visit the sick. He baptized all the children in danger of death and every dying adult who was interested in instruction.

He also cared for all the sick Mohawks and tortured Algonquin Indians he met. On one occasion, Father Jogues was told to tend a dying brave.

This man had tortured Father Jogues just months before. Now he was dying of a horrible disease that had covered him with foul-smelling sores. Although he could hardly stand the sight and the smell, Father Jogues nursed the sick man for two weeks.

In his year among the Mohawks Isaac Jogues had baptized seventy children and adults belonging to five different tribes, and he was content to remain among the savages as long as God should be pleased to keep him there.

During one of his trips to a Dutch settlement with some members of his master's household, Father Jogues was offered an opportunity to escape. It was a hair-raising experience in which he was bitten by a huge dog and spent almost a whole month lying on hard planks in a hot attic while his bitten leg swelled with infection. At last he was smuggled aboard a ship bound for France.

It was Christmas morning, 1643, when Father Jogues set foot on French soil. But he did not stay long in Europe. The wooded shores of his beloved St. Lawrence beckoned him to return. And return he did—but not without his human nature having to bend. He admitted to his superior, "My poor nature trembled as it remembered everything that had gone before. But our Lord, in His goodness, calmed it and will calm it still more. Father, I desire what our Lord desires — and I desire it at the peril of a thousand lives. How I would regret it if I lost such a wonderful opportunity, one in which I might be responsible if some souls were not saved."

Father Isaac Jogues did return to his Iroquois tribes. Some of his former captors were very happy to see him; others were not. Two days after his return, having received a supper invitation which he knew he could not refuse for fear of insulting his host, Isaac Jogues stooped to enter the low doorway of a longhouse. A tomahawk came crashing down on the missionary's skull, and Father Jogues crumpled to the ground, dead.

St. Isaac Jogues met the end that he had so desired — to shed his blood for his Lord and for the brothers that Christ had redeemed.

26

God's
big
zero

Our story opens in a wooded area near the Indian mission of Sainte Marie on the banks of Lake Huron. It was deep in the night of June 19, 1647, and a lonely figure lay next to a small campfire. Furtive arms of flame struck out to cut away the choking blackness. Noel Chabanel was restless; sleep refused to relieve him of his mental torture.

"I don't belong here!" his thoughts clamored. "How can I possibly have a vocation to this work? I loathe this place! Is it possible that after almost four years I've made so little headway!"

Noel jumped to his feet and paced savagely back and forth, wringing his hands until they ached.

"What can I do? My God! My God! Why have You abandoned me so?

"I should go back to France where I can be of some *real* use. I've failed miserably *here*. At least in France I'll be able to employ my talents fruitfully instead of wasting my life in this hole! Look at yourself, Noel Chabanel. Thirty-five years old, with nothing accomplished. It's true my superiors sent me here. But all I have to do is ask to return and, in the light of my failures, for sure they'll send me back."

The anguish in his soul reached insurmountable intensity. Completely exhausted by the struggle, Noel collapsed, his face pressed hard against the dirt. He wept.

Why was this a supreme moment in his life?

Noel Chabanel's refined nature passionately craved to devote his life to a civilized and cultured people. In New France, immersed as he was in a raw existence, he faced a daily crucifixion. According to human vision, he was a "zero." He—the one-time professor of six languages, keenly intelligent and energetic—had been unable to learn the language of the Hurons. The Gospel message that he had come here to convey to the natives spurted out in stuttering, grating sounds. The natives despised him for his apparent ignorance and inability to adapt to their language and customs. They called him the "palest of the pale faces."

"Oh," he moaned, "where is that fervor I had when I first came here? Where are those ardent desires that once filled my mind and heart? I have instructed not one convert; distributed not even one Communion; heard not a single confession. What is my priesthood for, anyway, at least *mine*, in this jungle?"

A cold sweat bathed his body as Chabanel labored under the tidal wave of depression engulfing him.

"Is there no escape? Ah, escape! That would ease the strain—and...be cowardly. But to stay on will drive me to madness! Why can't life be simple? Why does it engender so many pitfalls and blockades to happiness?"

Every sense and fiber of this young priest recoiled from the life he shared with the Indians. His nose and eyes stung and watered from the putrid stench and filth of the smoke-filled tents. His queasy stomach revolted from the insipid, greasy food. His ears and head pounded from the shrill screams and wails of children, quarreling squaws, and yelping dogs. His flesh burned in the unmerciful sun, deadened in the piercing cold, quivered under crawling lice and ticks, ached and agonized beneath crushing packs and endless journeys. Was there no relief? Everything tore at Father Chabanel's delicate nature. Added to these physical pains was the dreadful loss of courage. His fellow missionaries worked zealously, desired martyrdom, sustained torture and excruciating fatigue, and reaped consoling fruits for the cause of Christ. Noel, instead, did not yearn for martyrdom. He feared it. Yes, the very thought of suffering and torture, of being burned alive or tomahawked, completely terrified him.

"A coward—that's what I am," he groaned.

He was tried yet more. He prayed, but God seemed so far away. Not a drop of spiritual consolation did his ravaged spirit drink! All was dark within him and around him. The campfire had long ago sputtered out. How long he lay there, Noel did not know.

"My God, what *do* You want of me?" he cried out in anguish.

Then out of that darkness came a great light.

"God wants *me!* Not what I can or cannot do, but *me!* Dear Lord, I'm on the cross. Help me. With Your grace, I will not come down."

Grace did pour into the generous heart of the missionary and he raised himself up on his knees. Groping for the large crucifix in his robe, he pressed it to his lips. With determination, he voiced this heroic vow:

"My Lord Jesus Christ, You have willed me to be a helper of the apostles in this Huron vineyard. I am most unworthy of this call. But I trust in You and in the designs of Your holy will in whatever part I have in the conversion of the Hurons to the Faith. I, Noel Chabanel,...vow to remain here at my post until...*until the end of my life*, if my superiors so wish. Accept me, O Lord, as a *permanent* servant in this mission. Make me worthy of so sublime a ministry. Amen."

It was morning, June 20, 1647, the feast of Corpus Christi. Life in the forest and in the village stirred as the stars surrendered to a greater light. Noel would stay on at his work. With a firm step, he headed back to the village, back to what his flesh dreaded; back to what his will embraced. His vow did not remove the natural aversion that he felt (and that he would feel until his death), but it did make him stronger. Every new day would bring its fresh demands to donation. Yes, Father Chabanel could say Mass and baptize the sick and dying. He could give the example of fortitude of spirit and submission to the divine will. He could—and he would! For the next two years he accepted the monotonous routine of inglorious, humiliating circumstances of life.

Ceaseless labors awaited him, and, as always, the painful lack of privacy. Lack of pure drinking water left him constantly thirsty. Boiled corn paste, acorns and roots left him tragically underfed and weak. The glorious conquest of souls for Christ was not to be *his* glory; his would be the victory over himself in obscurity. In a letter to his brother back in France, Noel once wrote:

"As you have already read in our reports, 'The Relations,' Father Gabriel Lalemant merited the hon-

Here I am, O Lord;
I have come to do
Your will.

or of martyrdom. Only a month before, I was in the same settlement. (You were robbed of the privilege of being the brother of a martyr.) Father Lalemant had been assigned to relieve me since I was physically stronger, and I was sent to a more difficult mission. I was not worthy of the crown he won. My turn will come, if it pleases God, and if I try to live my own 'bloodless martyrdom in the darkness.'"

In the fall of 1649, Chabanel was sent to assist Father Charles Garnier in evangelizing the Petuns. As he said good-by he remarked to his spiritual director,

"Father Chastellain, I hope to *really* give myself entirely to God *this* time, *once and for all!*"

Later, Father Chastellain remarked to a passing priest at the mission, "I am deeply moved after speaking with that good priest. His former superior at Sainte Marie told me that Noel was sustaining a great interior struggle. Father Chabanel's voice and appearance just now were indeed those of one offering himself up as a victim. I don't know what lies in God's providence for him, but this I do know: God wants that man to be a great saint."

Noel himself confided to a friend, "I don't know what is happening to me or what God wants of me, but I feel death is not far off and I am not afraid. This state of mind is not from me for I have always been afraid."

At the mission of Etarita, Father Chabanel worked only a few weeks with Father Garnier. They were intense weeks, filled with greater hardships and sufferings than Noel had ever experienced up until that time. Then a sudden turn of events and the ever-widening danger from the warring Iroquois occasioned the recall of Chabanel to the main mission of St. Joseph. On Sunday, December 5, 1649, Father Chabanel celebrated Mass and embraced Father Garnier farewell.

"I am going to where obedience calls me.... I must serve God faithfully until death." Then he set off with a few Huron braves, and late in the afternoon reached the village of St. Matthias. Meanwhile, twelve miles away, at the mission he had just left, the Iroquois swooped down on their prey. Father Garnier was among the dead. Flames and a trail of smoke gave mute testimony to the slaughter. Chabanel stayed on for two more nights at the mission of St. Matthias and then started out again for St. Joseph's on December 7th. His party traveled more than eighteen miles over dangerous and difficult trails. Nightfall forced them to take refuge in a heavily wooded area near the river. The Hurons fell asleep right away, but Father Chabanel stayed awake and prayed. He was content. As never before, he was convinced that God wanted only his good will, his best efforts, and the dogged determination of never turning back. The temptation of turning back was always there, but he had prayed and continued to pray earnestly for perseverance.

At about midnight, Noel heard a confused murmur in the distance. The victorious whoops of Iroquois and the cries of their captives became more and more distinct as the war party drew closer and closer. Chabanel shook the Hurons from their sleep and they all fled, circling around the Iroquois and heading back to St. Matthias. But Noel was exhausted. Hungry and tired to the breaking point, he fell to his knees and sighed,

"Go on without me. It doesn't matter if I die. Life is a slight thing. Besides, the Iroquois cannot take paradise away from me."

The braves left him there and eventually reached St. Matthias to report what had happened. In the meantime, Father Chabanel hid in a clump of trees and passed the night alone. At sunrise, he set out again for the main mission of St. Joseph. He reached the shores opposite the island and looked with dismay at the swollen river. Just then a Huron stepped out of the brush. Smiling, he offered to take the priest across in his canoe. They had gone but a few yards when the Indian suddenly turned back. Without a word, he motioned for Father Chabanel to follow him into the woods. Perhaps he sensed danger? There in the gloom and loneliness of the forest, Noel Chabanel fell at the feet of his assassin. Tomahawked and scalped, his body was thrown into the river, never to be found.

Only two years later was the exact nature of Father Chabanel's death made known to the Jesuits at St. Joseph's, when the Huron apostate boasted of ridding the world of the despised priest out of hatred for the Faith.

Saint Noel Chabanel's martyrdom had been more extended and excruciating than that of any of his companions. Aversion, sadness, and disgust are more trying than anything. According to the world's standards, Noel was a failure. But God's standards are quite different!

light
in
the
darkness

It was early October, 1677, in the Indian village of Caughnawaga. Peaceful cornfields and vegetable gardens warmed themselves lazily in the afternoon sun. Interspersed with dark pines, the maples' foliage glowed in the flaming hues of early autumn.

A small canoe came darting across the great St. Lawrence and glided into a landing just below a mammoth wall of Canadian virgin forest.

As Kateri set foot on that unfamiliar soil, her heart jumped for joy. A large and beautiful pine-log church dominated the entire panorama. It was the first church that Kateri had ever seen. It must have been natural for her to believe that this pine-log structure rivaled the great European cathedrals of which she had heard the Blackrobes speak.

But far surpassing the grandeur of all the churches in the world was the beauty of this young Indian maiden's spirit. Pagans as well as Christians knew that Kateri Tekakwitha's exceptional virtue was rare among the Indians of her day. She puzzled many —even her closest friends—with her strange lifestyle. Yet no one could say she was not a real Mohawk through and through—a woman of her people, a lover of all that was good and beautiful in Indian life. Only when there was a question of displeasing God did Kateri depart from the traditional tribal customs, many of which were obnoxious even to some of the pagan Indians.

New and strange faces greeted the young woman on the landing at Caughnawaga. Suddenly Kateri felt the sharp sting of homesickness, and tears welled up to blot out the scene. The sudden realization that she had left her own tribe forever startled her. Now she would follow a new and unfamiliar way of life. As warm and friendly as the Christian Hurons tried to be in welcoming her, it was not without a touch of sadness that Kateri left all those who were near and dear to her.

During her first days in her new home, Kateri's thoughts wandered back over the events that had led her to decide to leave the Indian settlement of Ganawage, one of the capitals of the Mohawk world, and come to live at the town of Caughnawaga, the "village of prayer."

The drunkenness and wild excesses of her people had not made her despise them. No, daily she prayed to God: "Rawánniio, have mercy on my brothers. Disperse their darkness with Your wonderful light."

Kateri Tekakwitha was born in April of 1656 in the Mohawk settlement of Ossernenon, located in what is now upstate New York.

She was the daughter of the Mohawk warrior chief Kenhoronkwa and his kind and gentle wife, Kahenta—an Algonquian woman captured during a Mohawk raid on her settlement. Kahenta had been brought to Ossernenon, where her goodness irresistibly attracted the attention of Kenhoronkwa.

As Kenhoronkwa's wife, now enjoying complete freedom, Kahenta soon adjusted to Mohawk living, but her adjustment did not include adaptation to their warfare and orgies of torture. Unlike the people with whom she lived, Kahenta was Christian, and no Christian could ever condone the vices of these pagans and the outrages they committed, especially when under the influence of "firewater."

So it was that when God blessed the marriage of Kenhoronkwa and Kahenta with a baby girl—whom they called Tekakwitha—Kahenta's first thought was to instill in her child a knowledge of Rawánniio and the desire to practice Christian virtue. Although Tekakwitha was only four or five years old when both parents died, victims of a smallpox plague, the words and examples of her good mother had already made a lasting impression on her, an impression time would never soften.

Tekakwitha, too, contracted smallpox, but Anastasia, a Christian friend of Kahenta's, nursed her back to health. Until the end of her life, Tekakwitha bore the marks of the affliction: facial scars and partial blindness.

Iowerano, her uncle, and now the new chief, adopted Tekakwitha as his daughter and placed her in the care of two aunts. As Tekakwitha grew so too did her skill at craftmaking and her dependability in domestic affairs. Iowerano was very pleased with his niece in many ways.

Only one thing puzzled him. Tekakwitha was not like other girls her age; she kept apart and silent; very rarely was she seen at dances or village gatherings. The chief blamed it on many things: her inability to see clearly in sunlight, her pockmarked face, her natural timidity, and the suffering she had undergone as a child.

Whenever she could find free time, Tekakwitha would run off into the forest, throw herself down on her knees and beg Rawánniio for His help. Finally,

Blackrobes came to the village and Tekakwitha availed herself of their direction.

Father Pierron knew immediately that there was something unique in this young Indian maiden who, although unbaptized and uninstructed, was nevertheless deeply Christian in her manner of speaking and living.

Tekakwitha's one and only desire was to be baptized, but she had her uncle to cope with. He hated the Blackrobes; how would he ever consent to have a Christian living under his own roof?

Tekakwitha also realized that she was fast reaching a marriageable age and her uncle and aunts were already making plans regarding her future. She obeyed them in everything except their urgings to marry. Even in the face of ridicule and cruelty, she stubbornly refused to speak of marriage. Finally Iowerano realized the uselessness of arguing any further and left her alone.

Tekakwitha's determination soon won her another victory: Iowerano at last consented to her Baptism, and she began a long period of study. On Easter morning, April 18, 1676, she received Baptism and was addressed for the first time by her Christian name: Kateri (Katherine). For the next few months, Kateri spent her days working busily in her uncle's house and helping the needy of the village, including the aged and the sick. But she soon became the victim of calumnies and suspicions.

Father Pierron realized that it was no longer prudent for Kateri to remain among her people, and he suggested that she flee to one of the Christian Indian villages in Canada. It was not without terrible risks that the plan was carried out. Kateri's uncle was so upset by what he called "ingratitude" that she knew he would be capable of anything in his wrath. Yet, deep inside Kateri loved her uncle and knew

"O God, have mercy on my brothers. Disperse their darkness with Your wonderful light."

that he loved her and wanted only what he considered to be her good. As she slipped out of the house in the dead of night, Kateri could not help crying at the thought she might never see Iowerano again.

Two or three weeks later, after a long and arduous journey for herself and her companions, Kateri arrived at Caughnawaga, where she made many new acquaintances. The good Christian women of this town were overjoyed to welcome her. Three months after her arrival, on Christmas Day, Kateri made her First Holy Communion. She was a source of edification to everyone. Her days were spent in prayer and good works, in mortification and in the extreme penances that were her new-found source of joy.

But even here in Caughnawaga, Kateri soon found herself being urged to find a good husband. One day she went to see Father Cholenec, the village Blackrobe. Resolutely she told him of her decision to renounce marriage in order to love only Christ. "I would be happy to live in poverty, even in misery, for His love alone," she said. On March 25, 1679, the Feast of the Annunciation, Kateri confirmed her resolution with a vow of virginity.

Then, barely one year later, the young maiden lay on her deathbed. Her weakened body had finally succumbed to the tremendous penances she had been practicing. On Wednesday of Holy Week, April 17, 1680, Kateri went to meet that Jesus whom she had loved and for whom she had suffered so much. She was twenty-four years old. Fifteen minutes after her death, Father Cholenec was startled by the change that came over the young woman's usually scarred face. It was radiant and bright and completely unblemished. Kateri—an unbelievably pure light in a dark wilderness.

28

slave
of the
slaves
forever

The harbor of the white-walled city of Cartegena, Colombia, steamed in a blanket of tropical humidity in the summer of 1616. Boards creaked as three men made their way up a gangplank. On deck, a swarthy sailor pointed to an open hatch. Slowly, the three men descended the ladder which led down into the dark recesses of the slave galleon.

As Father Peter clung to the ladder, a wave of heat and stench overwhelmed him. Dizzy and sickened, he prayed for strength as he continued his descent. His superior, Father Sandoval, had already preceded him. Just a few rungs above, Teodoro, their black interpreter, followed.

Peter Claver reeled when he reached the bottom, where the odors stifled his breathing. Sweat poured down his face and he swallowed hard as his stomach churned with nausea. His thoughts shrieked wildly, "I need air—air!" He wanted to run back up the ladder. But shame shackled his feet. Had he not *prayed* for this opportunity to help the poor, unfortunate slaves?

Father Claver's eyes adjusted to the dim light and he faced a sea of human beings, lined up on different levels of shelves, all chained together. Ebony bodies, half starved, naked, bleeding, and feverish, stirred as the strange visitors approached. Peter looked long at their terror-stricken faces. Suddenly a thud and the jangling of keys diverted his attention. A sailor brushed by Father Claver, mumbling some sort of apologies about the slaves still being fettered. They should have been loosened of their bonds before the padres arrived....

In a corner, Father Sandoval had already bent over a lower-level bunk. He was pouring water on a man's head. The labored breathing indicated death's approach. Father Claver crossed the room, knelt and joined Father Sandoval in prayer as the poor dying man breathed his last. "We came not a moment too soon," sighed Father Sandoval.

For the next two hours the Jesuits and their companion ministered to the men and women in the ship's hold. They washed their feverish, caked bodies, soothed their wounds, quenched their thirst. Although the interpreter was needed to communicate words, the unfortunate bondsmen and women understood the language of love silently spoken by the gentle strangers. Soon fright and timidity lessened, and Father Sandoval gathered a small group around himself. He held aloft his large crucifix. Teodoro translated Father's simple statements: "This is Jesus Christ, who loves you very much and will take care of you. I, too, am your friend, and I will be back tomorrow to tell you more about Jesus."

Grateful hands reached out to stroke the arms and garments of the two priests and their interpreter as the three turned to leave. Tears filled Father Claver's eyes. "This is probably the first compassion these poor people have experienced in months," he thought. Back on deck, a long draught of fresh air cleared his head. He timidly broached the question, "Father Sandoval, what do you feel every time you approach a slave ship?"

Looking young Claver straight in the eye, the veteran missionary answered, "Son, every time I hear that another slave galleon has docked, and think of what I'll have to encounter, I tremble from head to foot."

A sense of deep reverence and awe for this man filled Father Peter's heart. He prayed that he, too, could be so heroic!

The following year, Father Sandoval was transferred, and Father Claver took over the full responsibility of working among the black slaves. He was a little apprehensive. He had only been an apprentice. How could he continue on all alone in a task that never ended? Over ten thousand slaves spilled into the city every year!

"Father Rector," he ventured, "with your permission may I look for some slaves to act as interpreters? The language barrier is the greatest obstacle; there are over sixty different dialects...."

Permission received, Father Claver set out immediately to find helpers. After a while, he had about fifteen well-trained interpreters.

Despite the enormous task, not only would Father Claver meet the slaves on board ship, he would also accompany them to the filthy, one-windowed slave sheds where the poor Africans awaited market day. Torn from their homeland and loved ones, the men and women from all parts of Africa responded to Father Claver's love with child-like simplicity. They could not doubt his love for them. His eyes soft with compassion, his body taut with fatigue, his hands calloused with work—all these proved that he loved them! Once Peter Claver had soothed their aching bodies, he taught them of Jesus Christ, of His love for them, of His own life of hard labor and suffering and execution on a cross. Father Claver told the slaves that they were not alone in their misery, that although coerced to serve human masters, they could be, through the waters of Baptism, children of God. Their often inhumane owners could never own their souls, could never steal them from God's hands, could never rob them of their personal worth in God's eyes. With eagerness and joy, at this good news, most of the African natives embraced the new-found Faith.

Father Claver kept track of each of the baptized. He visited them on the plantations, in the prisons, and in the hospitals and personally provided a decent burial for those who died.

After working among his beloved children for six years, he solemnly pronounced his final vows in the Society of Jesus on April 3, 1622. Signing his name to the official document, he added, "Peter Claver, Slave of the slaves forever."

The days and months flowed into years. When Father Claver was in his mid-fifties, a brother of the Society, Nicholas Gonzales, was assigned to aid him in his missionary work among the slaves. Nicholas was strong, young and generous. But many times his human nature quailed at the prospects of making the daily rounds with Father Claver.

One exceptionally humid and still day, the horrifying thought of the filth, sickness, and misery filled Nicholas with loathing. He performed his duties of sacristan with hands that flew and a mind that raced even faster! Maybe, he thought, if I just keep myself extra busy today, Father Claver won't call on me to accompany him. I can't do it any more!

Suddenly, through the thin ceiling, Nicholas heard a familiar voice ring out from the room directly above. "Nicholas! Nicholas! It's time to go. Come and give me a hand with this pack."

Reluctance quickened Nicholas' pulse and bathed him in a cold sweat. "Oh, my, now what am I going to do?" he desperately asked himself, as he pushed open the door to Father Claver's cell. Father Peter did not raise his eyes, but Nicholas could see a smile playing on his lips.

As the brother handed the various herbs, medicines, sweet cakes, and trinkets to the priest to be packed, he thought, How happy he is to go out every day, and I....

Soon the two were making their way to San Sebastian hospital. Brother Nicholas riveted his eyes on Father Claver's face. "How can a man, after some twenty years, keep on with this drudgery day after day with the same energy and enthusiasm?" he kept asking himself. "My own body constantly cries out with weariness and nausea...." Their arrival at the hospital increased his anxiety and he stared blankly into the eyes of the brother who answered the door.

Father Claver was the first to speak. "Good morning. We've come to serve in any way we can. I could sweep, and our good Brother Nicholas here could make beds.... Or...whatever else you might have for us to do." Father Claver's self-forgetfulness was contagious and a real stimulant. Suddenly, new vigor and inspiration surged through Brother Nicholas. He rolled up his sleeves, wrapped a white apron around his habit and headed straight for the wards. For two hours, he and Father Claver worked hard, barely noticing the sights, smells and sounds. They saw through it all to the image of God hidden beneath tortured bodies and feverish faces. A strong sense of peace and deep joy pervaded Brother Nicholas' soul as he and Father Claver walked home in the torrid afternoon heat. Somehow, love for others made everything easier.

Again scrutinizing the calm features of his teacher, Brother Nicholas decided that Father Claver was just so full of love that he didn't feel human weakness any more.

"He must be some superhuman being, untouched by selfishness or temptation," thought Brother Nicholas naively. "I wish I were made of the same stuff."

Little did Brother Nicholas know then of the interior battles waged by his confrere. Only later, much later, would he dip into the soul of the "slave of the slaves forever" and glean something of Father Claver's heroic self-conquest. No, Father Peter Claver was no superhuman being. In fact, he shuddered within himself at the repulsiveness of his tasks. He was sickened by his duty many times, but he *did* it anyway! Whenever he felt hesitation welling up inside, he would increase his acts of mortification and humiliation. He had to conquer his weakness! He would! For the next twenty years he pushed on, praying intensely, reducing his sleep to the minimum, though often he dragged himself home, faint with exhaustion. He sat in his stuffy confessional for hours on end, listening to the confessions of his beloved black children. He spent hours teaching catechism and traveling great distances—pleading, always pleading, for his dear slaves.

Many self-righteous men and even some members of his own community disapproved of Father Claver's activities. He was going too far! A tremendous wave of criticism threatened to submerge his work and bury it forever. Humbly, but fearlessly, Claver accepted what he felt was his due. Others could step on him, frustrate him, humble him, just so long as he could share a little in the fate of his brother slaves. Had he not vowed to be their slave forever? Had not Christ emptied Himself, taking the form of a slave?

In his little notebook, always carried over his heart, he had once written: "I must imitate the donkey. How does the donkey behave? When slandered it keeps silent; when forgotten, it is silent; no matter how much it is pulled, kicked or maltreated, it never complains. So must the servant of God be. I stand before You, my God, as Your donkey." These dispositions of a highbred Spanish gentleman, once an excellent student, were the fruit of much prayer and effort.

In 1650, Father Claver embarked on his last missionary journey through steaming jungles and swamps. He returned to Cartegena racked with fever and barely able to stand. He had contracted the plague. Although his life was spared, the disease left him a broken, old man, with partially paralyzed hands and feet and a body that trembled from the palsy.

For four long years, the intrepid missionary lay helpless in his bare cell. A young lad, Manuel, was assigned as a nurse to the priest. Rough and inconsiderate, Manuel caused untold sufferings to the gentle old man. Before bringing the tray to the invalid, he himself would eat the choicest parts of the meals prepared for Father Claver. One after another, Manuel would thrust the spoonfuls into the trembling mouth. Father Peter could not chew well and with pleading eyes would silently beseech his tormentor to stop.

"Hurry up, old man! Do you think I have all day?" Manuel would complain.

At Father Claver's pleas of "Later...later," the youth would set the food down on a stool, where it would remain for several days. None of the priests at the residence nor even faithful Brother Nicholas knew of Manuel's mistreatment of their revered confrere. But one day Manuel did not show up to help Father Claver dress to go to chapel for Mass. The patient pulled himself out of bed, fumbled and fell. Brother Nicholas heard the thud and ran upstairs, shocked and grieved.

"Wait until I get my hands on that Manuel and tell Father Rector how he neglects you!"

"No...no...please don't do that. The poor lad tries his best," pleaded Father Claver with tears in his eyes. "He mustn't be punished on account of me!"

Brother Nicholas knew it was useless to say anything further.

Shortly before Claver's death, Father Rector brought the former viceroy of Peru to visit the venerable missionary. As the distinguished gentleman left, he requested some sort of souvenir. Father Claver waved a trembling hand around his bare room and remarked, "But I have nothing to give you."

"Why not give your mission crucifix?" suggested Father Rector.

Father Claver hesitated a moment. He struggled to hide the pain he felt at this detachment and act of obedience. Shakily he removed the crucifix and handed it to his guest.

Later that evening Brother Nicholas noticed the missing crucifix and asked Father Peter about it.

Unbidden tears rolled down the heroic priest's sunken cheeks. "Forgive me, Brother. See how self-willed I still am. I deeply regretted parting with my crucifix. It has brought so much consolation to me all during my life...."

Brother Nicholas quickly turned and brushed away tears from his own eyes. "God is certainly asking the ultimate of His priest, right up to the end!" he murmured.

It deeply pained Father Claver to be so useless and to have others wait on him. Feeling that he could *still* do something, he requested and obtained permission to have his black children come to his room to receive the sacrament of Penance.

"Ah, Nicholas," he remarked one day, "it is good for the old donkey to be in harness again!"

Just before two o'clock of the morning of September 8, 1654, Father Peter Claver died without a sign or movement.

Word rushed through the city like a strong wind. It blew up the all-but-forgotten memory of the priest of the slaves. Suddenly everyone remembered—they remembered! They seemed to see him again as he embraced terrified blacks in the ship holds and slave sheds, as he cared for the sick and dying, as he walked fearlessly among the lepers. For nearly forty years he had been a friend and a father to the slaves. And after a life of selfless dedication, he had been helpless and forgotten in his own last years. But now they remembered, and the world would always remember St. Peter Claver, the slave of the slaves forever!

29

radiant
beggar

The door of the infirmary creaked open. Benedict Labre lay still, as a fever burned its way through his body. He heard the faint, restrained steps of a monk approach. Benedict turned his head slowly and looked up. Father Abbot placed his hand gently on the young man's shoulder and whispered, "We're going to move you, brother, to the laymen's infirmary. This will enable us to give you the best possible care."

Father Abbot continued to speak. Benedict's rambling thoughts raced around and around in his tortured head. Through the veil of fever he caught the words, "My son, God is not calling you to our order."

After a painful moment, twenty-two-year-old Benedict murmured, "God's will be done."

As the days passed and the fever raged, darkness enveloped Benedict's soul.

This had been his seventh attempt to enter a monastery of the Trappist or Carthusian order. What did God want of him?

He had such a yearning for the strictest and hardest life, such a burning thirst for victimhood, for a life of penance and expiation. He had torn himself from the warmth and joy of his parents' home, only to be denied the common life of the monks. Why was he continually frustrated? Every time he reached out for what he thought was God's will for him, he met with resistance, and it seemed to be God Himself resisting him.

But, despite the darkness that clung to his soul, and the throes of scruples that baffled his mind, Benedict trusted.

He believed in God's love, although he didn't feel its sweetness. With complete abandonment, he accepted the anguish. Acceptance made the burden lighter.

If God did not want him in the monastery, then Benedict would continue to search for God's will.

During Benedict's convalescence at the hospice, his serene abandonment and piety edified the brother infirmarian.

Benedict Labre left the hospice on July 2, 1770, weeping profusely as he bade farewell to his good brother monks. Abandonment would not lessen the pain of separation.

The young man joined the stream of pilgrims and beggars, and set out on the series of holy pilgrimages that were to be his life. From one shrine to another, he journeyed. He adored God and venerated His saints, seeking, always seeking, God's will. He felt that his vocation was to be a pilgrim, but only until he found the right monastery that would take him and keep him.

Little by little, the hardships of this new life made themselves felt. The rigors of his pilgrimages far surpassed any mortifications he had sought in the monastery. He had indeed found the hardest and strictest life for himself.

Lumped together with harmful or lazy parasites of society, Benedict bore all sorts of insults, stoning, and filth with a silence that amazed people.

His nature rebelled, of course. He was not lazy by any means, and proud and arrogant he could be. The son of hard-working French peasants and the oldest of fifteen children, Benedict Labre was proud of his heritage. Although his nature shuddered in the face of insults and his body quivered with lice, he tried to embrace all in a spirit of expiation and penance. His mission in life, vague at first, became clearer. Benedict Labre was to share the insults and blows rained on Christ in His passion and death.

Up mountains, down their craggy slopes, through marshes and swamps, Christ's beggar made his way to Rome. The Shrine of all shrines invited him with its irresistible pull. He made seven trips to Rome before deciding to live there. He went through the city daily, eventually becoming a familiar sight to everyone. Begging his food from charitable or not-so-charitable people, he slept wherever Providence provided.

Numbed by the cold, half starved, with clothes worn and tattered, unshaven, Benedict was looked upon as a madman by most. But those more sensitive to grace and virtue saw beneath the disheveled, dirty tramp to the Christ that lived therein. Many would tremble before him, overcome by the awesome sense of the presence of Christ.

The pilgrim spent hours in adoration before the Blessed Sacrament, unflinching, radiant. Always silent and recollected, he knew, too, how to say a good word to his neighbors and how to listen to their troubles.

Life for this pilgrim and beggar consisted of prayer, mortification and great love for God, obtained by grappling with temptation, doubt, obscurity, and darkness. It was a darkness announcing a greater light. Suspected for adhering to heretical Jansenistic practices, he instead came out most strongly against such practices. His obedience saved him from his scruples. "It is better," he said, "to go to Communion out of obedience than to stay away out of humility."

In April, 1782, Benedict confided to his confessor that he could not separate his meditations from one another. He contemplated the Trinity and oftentimes felt himself drawn up to the Trinity by God's power. He had painfully, slowly climbed the immense staircase of the interior life.

On Good Friday, the following year, he was seen at St. Ignatius' Church in Rome. Leaning on his stick, Benedict looked more emaciated and unkempt than ever before. Had he not appeared so happy, he would have been a terrifying sight. A radiant smile lit up his face.

Father Marconi, his confessor, observed the strange radiance. He later wrote of Benedict, "One had only to see him, even in his rags, to feel an unaccountable stirring of joy."

Benedict approached Father Marconi and the two talked a while. Then the pilgrim told the priest that he was free from all temptations. Marconi knew now that Benedict would soon reach the destination of all destinations. His pilgrimage was about over. As Benedict walked away, Father Marconi thought, "He is going to die of asceticism and charity." Struggles had been Benedict's life; tranquillity would come only at the time of death.

The following Thursday, Thursday of Easter Week, Benedict Labre collapsed outside the church on his way out from Mass. He was carried to a near-by house. In his semi-conscious state, the pilgrim, still a Trappist in spirit, asked to be laid on the ground. "You are tired, Benedict; you want to go to sleep," said the benefactor carrying him.

"Yes, I am tired, I want to sleep," whispered Benedict.

Those were the last clear words he pronounced. His faint, continued moaning mingled with the prayers recited by a priest who had been summoned.

Then peacefully, silently, the humble, thirty-five-year-old beggar reached his journey's end.

Only after his death was it learned that this tramp, so often beaten, stoned, imprisoned, and insulted — only because he was a beggar — was indeed a mystic, a giant of the interior life. God had sanctified him to show the world the value of prayer and virtue.

30

**Elizabeth of
old
New
York**

The raw November wind whistled through the cracks in the rough stone walls of the quarantine building. Elizabeth walked up and down the draughty room, trying to get warm, casting anxious glances at Will, who had been coughing even more than usual these last few hours.

Would it never end—this torment of waiting for clearance and release? How the young mother wanted a warm room for Will and little Anna where she could attempt to nurse her sick husband back to health! But the quarantine laws in Leghorn were severe in the early 1800's. Having heard of a yellow fever epidemic in New York, the port officials had been afraid that the handsome American businessman apparently so near death from tuberculosis was in reality bringing a far more contagious disease to the shores of Italy.

Will coughed and squirmed in the bed that his kind friends, Philip and Anthony Filicchi, had sent him. Eight-year-old Anna Mary, who had been sitting quietly on a bench, reading the Psalms to herself, reached out for the piece of cord that had tied her box of belongings. The child stood up and began to skip rope in order to warm herself. Elizabeth had often done the same in these last days.

"Betty!" called Will. Instantly Elizabeth was at his bedside.

"Let's say our service," murmured the sick man. "I'll feel less chilled afterwards."

As she took up her worn prayerbook and knelt down with Anna beside the bed, the young wife marveled anew at what a religious transformation had taken place within her husband. Will had hardly ever gone to church until just a few months ago. His lack of interest in religion had been the one real cloud in their joyous and devoted relationship. Other difficulties—the death of Will's father, the decline of his family's importing business to the point of bankruptcy, the illness of one after another of their five children, the death of her own father, and Will's steadily deteriorating health—all these had disturbed Elizabeth far less than her husband's lack of faith. And now that Will Seton had truly turned to his Savior, his devoted wife experienced a feeling of deep joy—even while suffering the privations of this chill *lazaretto*.

Devoutly, the little Episcopalian family held their daily prayer service, while the wind continued to howl through the fissures in the old, stone walls.

November merged with December, and one day Elizabeth Bayley Seton was able to write in her diary: "Five days more, and our quarantine is ended. Lodgings are engaged at Pisa...." And she went on to rejoice in the new-found faith of her William. "When I thank God for my creation and preservation," she wrote, "it is with a warmth of feeling I could never know until now: to wait on *Him* in my William's soul and body; to console and soothe those hours of affliction and pain, watching and weariness which, next to God, I alone could do; to strike up the cheerful notes of hope and Christian triumph, which from his partial love he hears with the more enjoyment from me, because to me he attributes the greatest share of them; to hear him, in pronouncing the name of his Redeemer, declare that I first taught him the sweetness of the sound — oh, if I were in the dungeon of this *lazaretto,* I should bless and praise my God for these days."

William's period of quarantine had been shortened, but it was already too late. He who had come to Italy in an attempt to stave off death from the family enemy, tuberculosis, died in Pisa only a few days after his release from the *lazaretto.* And Elizabeth, together with little Anna, was welcomed into the home of her husband's Italian friends, the Filicchis, whose kindness she was never to forget.

Philip and Anthony Filicchi and their wives admired Elizabeth Seton greatly. Her devotion to her God, to her husband and daughter and to the children she longed for beyond the sea had impressed them from the first. Now they tried to show her how to draw even closer to the God she loved so much.

And Elizabeth was ready. It has been said of her that she had a soul "naturally Catholic." She had always yearned, for example, for the Real Presence of her Savior in the Eucharist, and when she saw how ardently her new-found friends believed in this, she, too, found herself falling on her knees before the Blessed Sacrament as it was carried in procession in the streets.

When Elizabeth and little Anna—now called Annina—set sail for home the following spring, the young widow had already decided that she and her children were to enter the Catholic Church.

The joy of returning to New York and finding the children—Bill, Dick, Kitty and baby Bec—all happy and well, was marred by one of those sorrows with which her life's path was strewn from beginning to end—the death of a loved one. The one person whom Elizabeth had been sure would understand her intention to become a Catholic had been Rebecca Seton, her sister-in-law and "soul's sister." And with Rebecca's death from tuberculosis only a few days after Elizabeth's return, one of the loneliest periods in the young widow's life began.

No one seemed to understand her desire to become a Catholic. Some friends and relatives opposed it vehemently; others grew cool. Several did give financial help to the struggling family—which would have been destitute without these people and the Filicchis'—but Elizabeth strove to attain financial independence. Meanwhile a storm of doubts raged in her soul, and it was only after months of waiting that she made an act of utter faith and entered the Church.

It was March 14, 1805. A few days later she made her First Communion and exclaimed, "At last God is mine and I am His!"

Although the future seemed obscure at first, God's designs gradually opened up before her. Three and a half years after her conversion, Elizabeth said good-bye to New York, a city of fond memories for her.

There she had been born, the youngest daughter of Doctor and Mrs. Richard Bayley. There she had lived through the first and trying days of the new and independent nation. There, at the age of nineteen, she had married William Seton. There they had lived for ten loving, unforgettable years before his untimely death. There, Elizabeth left her heart....

Yet, as she and her children boarded a small ship bound for Baltimore, a spirit of hope and confidence began to surge through her. It was a new life, a new beginning.

"I am the happiest creature," she wrote, "in the thought that not the least thing can happen but by His will and permission."

Elizabeth was going to Baltimore at the request of Father Du Bourg of St. Mary's Seminary. For many years this priest had dreamed of opening a Catholic school for girls. Elizabeth Seton seemed to be just the right person for such an undertaking. She was young, courageous and full of faith and love of God. In addition, she was highly educated, refined and well-mannered, a practical and balanced woman.

So it was that Elizabeth Seton launched what was to be a vast undertaking of the Catholic Church in America: its parochial school system.

The poverty and obscurity of those first years would have discouraged anyone —anyone, that is, but Elizabeth Seton. A woman of her caliber and undaunted trust in God was certain to attract attention. And attract attention, she did. Other young women, inspired by her sublime ideals and spirit of prayer, soon came to join her in her work.

Under the guidance of Archbishop Carroll, Mrs. Seton and her followers formed themselves into a religious community first known as the Sisters of St. Joseph. A few years later, they changed the name of the ever-spreading congregation to the Sisters of Charity. Sisters of Charity! The name was a program in itself. Their long black dress, elbow-length cape and characteristic black bonnet soon became a familiar sight in schools, hospitals, orphanages, in fact anywhere the spiritual or corporal works of mercy had to be carried out.

Amid the consolations, however, Mother Seton still suffered tremendous personal trials. In the soft, brown earth of the Blue Ridge Mountains, she laid to rest Harriet and Cecilia, her two sisters-in-law who had come to join her, and later two of her own dear children: Annina and Bec.

In January, 1821, at the age of forty-six, Mother Seton herself lay dying. In her spiritual diary one finds the sentiments of her last months: "Thy kingdom come! Every day I ask my soul what I do for it in my little part assigned, and can see nothing but to smile, be patient, pray and wait before Him. Oh, my blessed God, Thy kingdom come!"

"Death! Eternity! Three wheels of this old carriage are broken down, the fourth very near gone; then with the wings of a dove will my soul fly and be at rest. Courage, hope, heaven!"

On the door of St. Patrick's Cathedral in New York City, one finds a large bronze relief of Mother Seton. It is entitled, "Daughter of New York."

Elizabeth Ann Seton belongs to each one of us. This is the land in which she was born, lived and died, the land she cherished, the land for whose people she mapped out a program of charity that is still alive, strong and growing.

In all things she followed the exhortation of the Divine Master:

"'You shall love the Lord your God
    with all your heart,
    with all your soul,
    with all your mind,
    with all your strength....
You shall love your neighbor as yourself.'"
(Mk. 12:30-31)

31

mystic
in
the
kitchen

Big-eyed and wondering, six-year-old Anna quietly followed her bustling mother from bedroom to kitchen to parlor, watching her pack item after item of the family's essentials into large bundles.

"What's happening, Mama?" she asked repeatedly. "What are you doing that for?"

"We are going away, Anna. Far away. We will go to live in another city called Rome."

"But why, Mama?"

Mama Gianetti smiled down at her inquisitive daughter. "Just because," she soothed, as she hugged her tightly. "Now, Anna, take these clothes in to Papa. He's waiting to pack them into the trunk."

The young mother's smile quickly faded to a preoccupied frown, however, as she watched her daughter skip from the room.

"To Rome...for what?" she wondered.

Her husband had been an apothecary here in Siena, but his policy of too-easy credit had recently cost him the entire business. "We'll make a fresh start," he had promised her. "You'll see...I'll find a nice position with a steady income, and before you know it, we'll be all settled again!"

Signora Gianetti fervently hoped—and prayed—that it would be so. It would be so hard to pull up roots, especially when she didn't know what to expect at the end of the trip.

The year was 1775. The hustling city of Rome managed to find room for the newcomers in one of its poorer sections—a sort of "lower middle class" area. Signor Gianetti took up employment as a butler with one of the noble families of the city. It was a position which kept his own family in clothes and sufficiently fed, but certainly would never make them rich, or even "well-off." Signora Gianetti was content however.

"It will mean plenty of hard work," she told herself, "but there's nothing impossible about that. And besides, we have a home now."

Happily she set to the task of raising her lively little daughter. Anna Maria was soon enrolled in a small school nearby. Daily she would scamper out the front door, waving over her shoulder, and be off to more learning adventures. When Anna was back in the afternoon, Mama Gianetti would waste no time. She wanted to be sure her daughter grew up to be a "proper young lady." Gradually she introduced her to the secrets of cooking and housekeeping—the way to test the spaghetti and measure the right amount of oregano for the sauce, and the art of patching a frayed shirt sleeve. To her mother's pride, by the time she was twelve or thirteen, she had become a real help around the house.

"In fact," her mother would joke, "one of these days I'm just going on a vacation! Anna Maria will take care of everything!"

The family's financial situation was not, however, on the same upswing as Anna Maria's housekeeping. It became gradually clearer that with their growing number and rising prices, more income definitely was needed.

Mama Gianetti thought over the situation carefully. She didn't like the idea of having to stop her daughter's schooling, but she couldn't see any other solution.

"Anna," she said pensively one evening as they cleared away the supper dishes together, "Papa and I need your help."

"Oh, sure, Mama! What can I do?"

"Well, it won't be too easy.... I know how you like school.... But you're a big girl now, and I think you can take bigger responsibilities. Papa has obtained a position for you as a maid to Donna Maria Sera at the Palazzo Maccarani."

Anna's eyes opened wide. A flurry of thoughts whirled through her mind. No more school—she would miss that, she knew, but she was grateful for what she had had. She was rather stunned at the thought of being in the company of real "ladies," but Papa would be near, since he worked there, too. Soon the thrill of anticipation outweighed any apprehension she might have felt!

"I'll be able to help the family out, too, won't I, Mama?"

Signora Gianetti nodded, smiling in quiet relief. "Yes, Anna, and you know how we need it! Besides, I think you'll be able to learn quite a bit, and meet many wonderful people!" She smiled again and turned back to the dishes, satisfied that the matter was settled.

Anna quickly learned the basics at the Palazzo; her evident knack for serving, her thoughtfulness of others and her sincere courtesy soon put her on a par with many of the more experienced servants — especially in her mistress' eyes. So it was that Anna Maria often accompanied the cortege when the Maccaranis went visiting.

The young girl could not help but observe the grand women of society at close range. She saw their mannerisms, habits of dress and the hours of beautifying spent before the mirror. All in order "to make an impression" and insure a "good time."

As the years slipped by, Anna quickly approached womanhood. She began to take notice of the petite figure behind Donna Maria in the mirror at the dressing table. She became more and more conscious of her own good looks, and began to pay close attention to how she walked, how she talked, what she wore, how her hair was done. Her vanity even became a little more exaggerated than that of most girls in their late teens, and Mama Gianetti realized it. But the observant mother also saw that Anna Maria did not seem to be losing her winning disposition. The young woman still proved as generous, loving and thoughtful as always...so Mama Gianetti said nothing.

But Anna Maria was becoming quite taken up with herself, and, as she approached twenty, she became aware of the fact that someone *else* was, too! His name was Dominic Taigi. He was a footman for the Chigi family, who were friends of the Maccarinis.

It wasn't long before Mama Gianetti noticed a particular flush in her daughter's face when she spoke of the Chigis and a certain footman.

"Come now," Anna's mother prodded one evening in a gentle, motherly way. "Tell me about him."

It was all Anna needed. Everything rushed out in a stream of breathless explanation. "His name is Dominic, Mama. He's tall and good-looking, I know he goes to church, and...I think he likes me," she ended softly.

"Well, my dear," Mama smiled, "perhaps he'd like Papa and me, too, then. Everyone always says you're just like your parents!"

Mother and daughter laughed happily together.

The "liking" grew mutually. The Gianettis felt it was a "good match." And a date was set for their daughter's marriage.

The day after the celebration of the Epiphany in 1790, the church of San Marcello was abuzz with a crowd of well-wishers. The wedding was a small one, as neither the bride nor the groom was terribly well-off. But nothing could dampen the joy in those two young hearts.

Dominic Taigi loved his beautiful bride, and in the months following their wedding, he encouraged her already strong desire to "pretty-up." Together they enjoyed nice clothes and good times — in much the same fashion, Anna reflected, as she had often seen the "great ladies" do, though on a smaller scale.

It was just after their first child was born that Dominic began to sense a change in his wife. Often he would find her deep in thought as she cuddled that tiny bundle. And many times there was an almost forced enthusiasm as they prepared for a party.

What Dominic did not and could not know was that a profound stirring of God's grace was making itself felt in Anna's soul. She had begun to ponder the miracle of life she saw in her little one's tiny fists, sparkling eyes and toothless smile. The shallowness of her preoccupation with extravagant clothes stood out in glaring contrast to the simplicity and genuine beauty she saw mirrored in that precious little life entrusted to her. The Creator of that life must be tremendously more beautiful and loving, she thought.

She began to slip into church for a visit more often—as long as nothing at home was neglected. Almost instinctively she took to dressing more simply and being less showy.

One Sunday morning it all came to a head, when Dominic bellowed at her, "You're not wearing *that* to church, are you?!"

Anna looked down at her dress and mentally braced herself. She knew from past experience that her husband's temper could be violent once it was touched off. "It's not a *bad*-looking dress, is it, Dominic?" She tried to soothe him with her calm.

"No—but you've had it for *ages!* You've newer ones, fancier ones.... You know I like you to really stand out! And besides, it's not just *this*. You've been acting so strange lately...less jewelry, plain clothes...."

His voice trailed off. Now he was puzzled more than angry, and Anna took the opportunity of the lull to try to reassure and explain.

"Dominic, remember that I am your wife first of all and always. I never want to shame you or displease you, believe me. But, you see, lately I've felt differently about a lot of things.... Dominic, love me for what I am, not for elaborate clothes or necklaces. After all, the Madonna was the most wonderful woman who ever lived, and her beauty was not in any jewels, but in her soul. I want to be more like her, Dominic, and be truly beautiful for you and for God."

Her husband softened. He loved his Anna and, though he did not understand, he decided he would try to go along with this, to please her. Anna herself was marveling at her "victory"—she hadn't expected him to agree so easily. She murmured a quiet "Thanks be to God," and said cheerfully,

"Well, shall we be off to church, now, dear?"

He smiled down at her and nodded.

Time flew and gradually the modest Taigi home filled with new young faces. There would be seven in all. Anna loved and cared for them with all her might. They and her husband were her first concern, and she wore herself out for them.

Daily she made it a point to be home from the market or bakery in time to greet Dominic as he returned from work. She always had his chair ready, and a cool drink waiting for him. She never failed to ask about his day—the problems, the anxieties, and the pleasant events, too. She listened to him, was interested, and—so Dominic decided—made him feel like a million.

Her children, too, were constantly on her mind. Somehow she always managed to find time to be with them, to teach them their prayers, to join in their fun, to devise intriguing games, and, simply, to be a real mother.

There was still another facet to Anna Maria's full life, though. From that very first year of her marriage, there had developed a dizzying crescendo of contact with God. So much seemed to be happening at once that it had her puzzled.

Why did God choose me? she often thought. I'm just an ordinary housewife with a husband and family to care for. I can't spend all day in church— not even the greater part of it. And yet He has set me on fire, put this burning desire for Him in my soul.... It seems it will never be quenched! But I'm only Anna Taigi—not Catherine of Siena!

What Anna *did* know was that she had to become a saint—but wasn't everyone supposed to do the same? She hadn't counted on all the "extras" that the Lord seemed bent on showering on her.

Often He would show her future events of no small magnitude. Long before they occurred, she knew of such happenings as the seizure of Rome by the French in 1797 and the captivity of Pope Pius VII under Napoleon. Though she had no desire to be "special," she would obediently reveal what she was told to the proper people and then return quietly to her housework.

"I only want Dominic to have a simple, loving wife, always there when he needs her," she would exclaim, and she meant it heartily.

But the Lord continued to show His favor. He frequently made His presence so intensely felt that it would take Anna's breath away.

One afternoon one of her daughters was coming in from the garden with an armload of squash to clean. She stopped outside the kitchen door, startled at her mother's tone of voice. There hadn't been anyone with Anna before....

"Enough, Lord, enough!" Anna was pleading. "Can't You see that I have supper to prepare now? There are eight hungry people who have to eat soon, Lord." Wonderingly, her daughter tiptoed in to see Anna leaning against the cupboard as if she were very tired; her back was turned.

"Here are the squash, Mama," the girl finally ventured. Anna Maria stood up immediately. Turning, she smiled and said, "Good, dear, bring them here to the table and we'll clean and cut them." Everything seemed normal and the young girl shrugged her shoulders.

Anna tried as much as possible to conceal these extraordinary experiences, but even when she couldn't, it was clear that she neither expected nor wanted any fanfare, even from her children. This is borne out by the comment her eldest daughter, Sophie, made on another occasion.

Sophie had been cleaning in the bedrooms one morning and was on her way to shake out the dust-cloths, when she came upon her mother sweeping

"...You are the way which I must follow; the perfect model which I must imitate."

the kitchen. However, Anna and her broom were floating a good few inches off the floor, Anna's face radiant in ecstasy! Sophie was startled at first, but then her practical streak came to her rescue.

"Mama!" she exclaimed, "Please come down! There's no dust up there at all!"

Not everything was sweetness for Signora Taigi, however. As the years went by she was plagued with severe migraine headaches which became more and more frequent. These, added to nearly constant arthritic pain, left her hardly a moment of physical peace. But Anna Maria's will power had been steadily strengthened through self-discipline and prayer, and she refused to let up in the least in fulfilling the continual demands placed on her as mother and wife.

It was no real surprise to her family, then— though certainly a cause for sorrow—when one morning in October, 1836, the sixty-seven-year-old wife of Dominic Taigi could no longer muster sufficient strength to leave her bed. For nine long months she struggled to live. Then, early in June, 1837, Anna felt she would not have to fight much longer. Knowing that she would soon be seeing her Lord "face to face," she called her children around her. Taut with emotion, Dominic stood in the background.

Anna's voice had become raspy and hoarse. Everyone leaned close to hear her.

"Love the Lord always," she whispered. "Nothing here on earth can compare with what He has prepared for us.... And love Mary, the Madonna. She will be a mother to you when I am gone."

Her voice trailed off into silence. A faint smile flickered on her lips as she gazed slowly around the circle of faces — her children. Then, as silently as a spent candle gives up its flame, Anna Maria was gone.

For forty-eight years she had been a wife and mother, in the fullest sense of these words. No one could have ever found fault with her running of the Taigi household; she had never been missing whenever her husband or her children had needed her. Yet she had still found time to draw close to the Almighty to a degree that few reach. As God had revealed to her confessor nearly fifty years before, Anna Maria had proved that it *was* possible to be a mystic in the kitchen.

O Jesus, You are the Way which I must follow; the perfect model which I must imitate. Grant that I may live of faith. Make me Your ardent apostle in my vocation, so that in presenting myself at the judgment I may be found similar to You.

32

only
God
could
stop
her

One day in 1792, when the violence of the French Revolution was at its height, a howling mob rushed on the chateau in the village of Chamblanc and set it ablaze. As the fire devoured the imposing building, a youthful figure could be seen silhouetted against the flames. A girl was running for safety, her arms clasping the monstrance and sacred vessels she had rescued from the chateau's blazing chapel. Some of the men began to run after her, but the thirteen-year-old's swiftness was no match for the slower gait of the weapon-laden revolutionaries, and Anne-Marie Javouhey escaped.

"Curse that sly, little tomboy!" one man roared. "She's the same one I saw two weeks ago huddled in a boat with a fugitive priest!"

"And she's the one who tips off every priest in the district!" growled another marshall. "Just when they're almost in our grasp, she pulls another trick escape. She sends her younger brothers and sisters into town as spies to check out the whereabouts of the exiled priests that have returned and then arranges for Masses in barns and attics under the pretext of throwing parties! Why, my men have even seen her teaching catechism to the village children while walking up and down the roads or sitting in the meadows; actually they haven't heard her, but they can tell what she's doing because she's very evasive when they question her. If I ever get my hands on that brat, I'll throw her in prison and give her a beating she'll never forget!"

"Wait a minute, Simon, you shouldn't arrest a child of thirteen. Come on, let's go celebrate the burning of the chateau."

Anne-Marie, or Nanette as she was more commonly called, continued her heroic adventures. She even persuaded her reluctant father to shelter a priest, Father Vincent Ballanche, in their attic. Balthazar Javouhey ordered everyone to leave Father Ballanche alone and to go on with life as usual. But any normal activity was completely out of the question.

A constant stream of people flowed in and out of the Javouhey home, seeking the help of the good priest.

All this traffic worried Balthazar. It was sure to attract the attention of the deputies and endanger himself, his wife, and their six children. Besides all this, Nanette was hounding him for permission to become a nun. Why, she would drive him crazy with that foolish idea of hers! A nun? Preposterous! She was a mere child, and the times were all but conducive to convent life! Besides, he could not lose his pride and joy, his Nanette, his little girl.... Balthazar longed for the day when things would return to normal and Nanette would forget that "bee in her bonnet" and settle down as any young woman should. As it was, she was courting danger and would bring catastrophe down on all of them if she wasn't careful.

One night, when Father Ballanche had come down from his attic refuge to spend some time with the Javouhey family, the household jumped up at the sound of pounding on the door.

"Open up in the name of the Republic!"

"Quick, Father Vincent," Nanette whispered, "into the closet!"

Father Ballanche dashed into the coatroom and pulled the door shut, but the latch didn't catch.

Nanette opened the front door. "Good evening," she said.

"Where's the priest?" demanded the deputy. Three other men stood behind him.

"What priest?" Nanette responded innocently.

"I know he's here!" the deputy shouted. "And you, Balthazar Javouhey, are under arrest for harboring him. You will get the man and both of you will come with me to the village."

Laughing, Nanette replied, "But, sir, my father can't produce a priest out of thin air. If you think there is one here, you're free to search the house. Please come in."

Balthazar cast a worried glance in Nanette's direction.

"Mind your own business, young lady," the deputy snapped. "I have enough information on you to send you to the guillotine. Keep out of this!"

"As you please, sir," Nanette soothed. "But do come in; you're letting in the cold."

The four men stepped inside and Nanette closed the door. The floor creaked and sank a little beneath their weight; the closet door swung open. Panic flashed across the faces of the Javouheys as they stood by, helpless. The deputy caught their look of alarm. Grinning, he walked toward the closet.

Nanette stepped forward. She smiled and offered, "Allow me to take your coats." Turning to her

father, she added, "Daddy, prepare some wine for
our guests. They must be very cold. This is no weather to be out looking for anyone. After we've chatted
a bit we can help these good men search the house.
If there is a priest here, I would like to talk to him."

By this time, Nanette had taken the coats, hung
them in the closet and shut the door firmly. She
looked expectantly at her father.

"The wine, Daddy."

"Oh, yes, the wine," Balthazar repeated as he
snapped out of his daze.

"Never mind the wine," ordered the deputy.
"If there were a priest here tonight, you wouldn't
be so hospitable. Fetch my coat, girl, and be quick.
Make no mistakes about it, my friends, I'm keeping
a watch on this house. So don't try any funny business."

Nanette nudged her brother Pierre and signaled
him to help the men. The boy crossed the room, took
the coats and left the closet door wide open.

The deputy eyed the seventeen-year-old girl
and the open closet. Nanette returned a steady gaze.
Shaking his head, the deputy said, "Young lady, you
are very brave and, I might add, very clever. What
I've heard about you must be true. If I didn't have
my orders, I'd let you keep the priest. Good night."
The door closed after the four men, and their foot-
steps receded. A sigh of relief escaped everyone in
the room. Father Vincent stepped out of his hiding
place and looked long at Nanette.

"You saved my life tonight," he said.

With her same steady gaze, Nanette responded,
"There's a way you can save mine, Father Vincent."

Two evenings later, Father Ballanche and
Nanette argued with Balthazar Javouhey. But they
got nowhere. "No, Father Vincent," declared Balthazar, "I will not permit my daughter to go to the

convent. She's too young to know her mind. I can't let her go; I won't!"

There was a deadlock for months.

But with kindness, calm and a disarming smile, Nanette cut the rope of Balthazar's paternal possessiveness. He grimly surrendered to his daughter, who had inherited his own stubbornness. On November 11, 1798, Anne-Marie Javouhey took private vows. She was to live as a sister at home.

Nanette dedicated herself almost exclusively to teaching the Faith to the villagers and arranging for them to receive the sacraments as frequently as circumstances permitted.

On one occasion, with the alibi of a picnic, she gathered all the children of the village who had not received First Communion and took them to an old, abandoned shrine in the forest. There a priest was waiting, as well as some of the parents. Everyone was visibly moved by the First Communion ceremony. Word of it spread among the families of the village and bolstered their faith.

In 1800, the new regime in France permitted pastors to return to their parishes. When Father Paul Rapin came back to Chamblanc, he thought he would find his parish in complete chaos. Instead, he discovered a very fervent flock. The amazing fact was chiefly attributable to the work of one teen-age girl.

Deeply impressed by Nanette's fervor and hearing of her desire to enter the convent, Father Rapin talked to Monsieur Javouhey about giving his permission. Reluctantly, and hoping against hope that his daughter would not last, Balthazar finally consented.

After a few months of convent life, Anne-Marie returned home. Balthazar felt relieved. After all, he had known she wouldn't make it. He had been right all along. It was his victory, or so he thought. Then one day Anne-Marie made a startling announcement. From her father it evoked the usual response.

"You foolish girl!" Balthazar stormed. "What do you mean you're going to *found an order?* Who put that crazy idea into your head?"

"God did," Nanette answered softly. "One night last month while I was in the convent, a bright light filled my room. I saw a whole group of children with different-colored skins. Some were black, some were bronze colored, and some were yellow skinned. A sister stood in the midst of them and said to me, 'These are the children God is giving you. You are to found an order. My name is Teresa and I will be your patroness.' Then the whole scene disappeared. I had never known that there were people with different-colored skin, so I asked my confessor if there were and he said, 'Yes, in Africa, America, and the Far East.' I'm sure that this is what God wants me to do."

Although Nanette was confused as to how to begin, one thing was clear to her: she had received a direct call from God. With characteristic Javouhey headstrongness, she embarked on her adventure.

Nanette spent the next six years in undertaking what seemed one failure after another. Lack of food, utter poverty, eviction from rented buildings, and financial bankruptcy spoke of defeat. But every time things looked most hopeless, Nanette turned to God and to the only man on earth who she knew would help—her father. Despite his gruff, stern manners, Balthazar Javouhey would do anything for his oldest daughter, and she knew it. Balthazar finally purchased a large house in Cluny where there was sufficient room and opportunity for the sisters and the children they taught. By this time Nanette's three younger sisters had joined her, along with four other women. They filed into St. Peter's Church in Chalon on May 12, 1807, to pronounce the religious vows of poverty, chastity, and obedience before the bishop. Sister Anne-Marie Javouhey was twenty-eight at the time.

As members of the new congregation of the Sisters of St. Joseph of Cluny, the sisters dedicated themselves to the instruction of children. The convents and much-needed schools of the Sisters of St. Joseph of Cluny sprung up all over post-revolutionary France. Sister Anne-Marie wondered, though, when she would take care of the "black children" God had given her so many years before. Finally the time came. First to Reunion, an island in the Indian Ocean, then to St. Louis in Senegal, Africa, then to French Guiana in South America, Mother Javouhey sent her daughters.

After the expanding congregation was well on its feet, Mother Javouhey herself went to the mission lands until circumstances called her back to France. All the while, she had to overcome countless and almost insurmountable obstacles, within and without the order. When she needed help, she would ask people she knew. If they did not help, she would go to others, and to others and on even to King Louis-Philippe himself, until she accomplished what she felt God wanted her to do.

This stout little woman, with pink cheeks, sparkling eyes, and soft voice, was always in command of the situation. When it came to doing God's will, nothing, but nothing stood in her way; not even the greatest personal sacrifice. She thrived on obstacles.

Everyone recognized Nanette's virile strength. On one occasion, after Mother Javouhey had finished speaking with King Louis-Philippe, the monarch turned to those near him and stated, "Make no mistake about it, my friends: Mother Javouhey is a great man!"

During the uprising of 1848, when the streets of Paris witnessed riots and bloodshed, Mother Javouhey was seen going from one barricade to another. The soldiers recognized her, greeted her with jokes, and shouted to their comrades, "It's General Javouhey! Pass, General!"

The strength of Nanette's character was especially seen in her relations with Monsignor d'Hericourt, Bishop of Autun. He had rashly misjudged Mother Anne-Marie; he even denied her the consolation of the sacraments for two years!

But the valiant foundress never uttered a word of anger against the bishop. Nor would she permit anyone else to criticize him in her presence. She kept repeating, "Let us pray for His Excellency, for in reality he is a great benefactor; he has afforded us an opportunity to suffer for the Lord."

In March, 1851, Mother Javouhey collapsed in the corridor leading to her office at the motherhouse. She had driven herself harder than ever in these last years, in order to accomplish as much as possible. Now she would continue to work from her sick-bed for the few months still remaining to her.

On the evening of June 15, Sister Anne-Marie spoke with her sister Claudine, who was now the new Mother General. They discussed plans for the forthcoming trip to Rome to obtain papal approval for their order. Claudine urged Nanette to rest so that she would be strong enough to make the trip.

Anne-Marie looked at her sister for a moment and then sighed, "Oh, no. I'm not going to Rome. I have another trip to make which I must make alone."

Claudine grew apprehensive and went to summon a priest. When she returned to the sick room, Nanette was trying to get up. Easing her older sister back into bed, Claudine whispered, "You must rest."

"Yes," Nanette murmured. And she rested in God.

33

light
in the
grotto

The morning was cold and damp. A thick fog blanketed the little town of Lourdes, France. In the Soubirous home, Mama Louise was cleaning a few vegetables for the thin soup that was to be their noon meal.

"It certainly is chilly this morning," she thought to herself. It usually didn't take much to heat up the shabby, little one-room dwelling that the Soubirous called home, but Mama Louise sighed, as she glanced at the fireplace. There wasn't a stick of wood left on the pile—and how she hated to send her daughters out in weather like this. But the girls saw her glance and were quick to understand.

"We'll go!" offered twelve-year-old Toinette. By "we" she meant herself, her friend Jeanne Abadie, and Bernadette.

"Bernadette," protested her mother, "you shouldn't go out; your cough might come back again."

"Don't worry, Mama, I'll put on my cloak and cap so I won't be cold."

Mama Louise nodded her consent. Her gaze remained fixed on the door after the three had gone. "Can it be true?" she thought worriedly. "My poor little Bernadette...the whole *town* is talking about her so-called "Lady." She's always been such a level-headed girl.... It's all so strange...." Mama Louise sighed again and turned back to her vegetables.

While Lourdes buzzed with rumors and ridicule, Bernadette Soubirous went about her daily duties just as usual. She was an ordinary poor girl — small for her age of fourteen — who lived in an impoverished little room with her parents, brothers and sister. She hardly seemed to have been favored by heaven.

Francis and Louise Soubirous and their children — Bernadette, Toinette, John and Justin — shared that one small room, which had once been a jail cell, with its humble furnishings of three beds and a chair.

The air in that room was thick enough to make anyone choke, and for Bernadette, whose asthma already made breathing difficult, it was often unbearable. At times she would stand by the barred window and gulp great draughts of the fresh, clean air which blew down from the Pyrenees Mountains. At night she could not do this without disturbing the family, so she would lie awake next to her sister Toinette, suffering as silently as possible, but letting a cough escape her now and then.

It was especially at times like these that Bernadette fingered her worn rosary, and tried to absorb her thoughts in its mysteries. She enjoyed this prayer in a special way. It was simple and *so* human! During each decade she recalled one of the main events in the lives of Jesus and His Mother, Mary. By the time she finished fifteen, she had pondered the joyful, sorrowful and glorious points, from the Annunciation of the angel to Mary, through the Passion of Jesus and His glorious resurrection, all the way to the Queenship of the Mother of God.

Her asthma still clutched at her throat at the end of the rosary, but somehow it didn't bother her so much. The long hours of waiting for sleep did not drag so and she grew ever closer to her heavenly Mother. In her uncomplicated and unassuming way, Bernadette had never realized just *how* close that Mother was, until one wintry morning....

It all began on February 11, 1858. Bernadette, Toinette and Jeanne were gathering firewood, as they often did.

After a short walk from home, the girls came to the River Gave at the grotto, or cave, of Massabielle. Toinette and Jeanne saw some sticks on the far side and waded across to get them, squealing because of the iciness of the water.

"Please throw some stones in so that I won't get my feet wet," Bernadette called. "Mama wouldn't want that!"

Jeanne, however, retorted, "You're such a nuisance! Stay where you are if you don't want to cross!"

As the bells of St. Peter's Church pealed out the Angelus, and its echoes died away among the hills, Jeanne and Toinette quickly gathered the bits of wood which lay near the river and moved farther off. Bernadette was left alone.

At first, she threw stones into the stream in order to make a crossing, but the attempt failed, so she decided to take off her shoes and wade over as the others had done. Just then, she thought she heard a rumble of distant thunder—or was it a sudden gust of wind? Bernadette glanced about. There were no storm clouds; nothing stirred. I must have been mistaken, she thought, and bent down once again to remove the shoe.

But there was that same sound! This time Bernadette stood up and looked about intently. What was happening? On the slope before her a wild rosebush was tossing violently as if caught in a gale. Everything else was still.

As Bernadette stared, a beautiful young Lady appeared, and stood in a golden mist right above the rose bush. Bernadette felt numb. She rubbed her eyes, closed them and reopened them, but the Lady was still there. That warm smile told Bernadette that this *was* real, after all! Quickly she pulled her rosary from her pocket, and began to pray.

Bernadette's mother was unusually serious later that afternoon, when the news of the Lady slipped out. "You must get these ideas out of your head, Bernadette," she decided. "And, you are not to go back to Massabielle again!" The joy of Bernadette's meeting with the Lady was already mixed with pain—her parents' disapproval. And soon it was not only her parents; many of the townspeople joined in as well.

"It's almost like the rosary," Bernadette thought. "There are the happy things...and the harder things." But, actually, what the people thought did not bother Bernadette so. The most difficult thing was being refused permission to return to Massabielle.

As she lay awake that first night her only thought and desire was for the Lady at the grotto. The beads slipped through her fingers slowly. Deep inside she knew God would open a way.

And ways did open. With each obstacle came an opened door so that she was able to return to the Lady eighteen times in all.

The stormy events surrounding Bernadette and her Lady are well known: the disbelief, and condescending pity of many who believed her to be a victim of illusions, and most frightful of all, her difficult interviews with certain city officials.

Her strength of will never flagged, however. After all, she would think to herself, the Lady hadn't promised happiness in this world, but "in the other." She drew her stamina from the rosary and the Lady of the Grotto, who later revealed herself to be "The Immaculate Conception," the Virgin Mother of God. The rosary had been given by this same Mother hundreds of years before to the great St. Dominic, and had been approved and encouraged by the Holy Fathers down through the years.

Bernadette was not, perhaps, aware of the history behind the smooth beads in her hand. But of the power of intercession they represented—this she knew better than her own name. And she never ceased clinging to it for support.

The message of the Virgin to Bernadette, and through her to the world was a simple one, a timeless one. "Pray and do penance for sinners." For the rest of her short life, Bernadette strove to live this mandate of the Lady. Not long after the final apparition she went to live at the local convent of the Sisters of Charity and worked as their maid. Nothing contented her more than remaining small and hidden. Eventually she was accepted at Nevers as a postulant in the Order, and was assigned to washing pots and pans in the kitchen. So completely unlettered was this girl from Lourdes, that there was even question about admitting her to religious profession. But her virtue was outstanding, and so it was decided that "as a favor" she would be allowed to make her vows and be assigned to help in the infirmary.

After two years, she was given the position of sacristan, a duty she loved very much since it obliged her to spend many hours in chapel. However her health, which had always been poor, was now failing rapidly. Soon she returned to the infirmary, but now as a patient. In her months of trial, both spiritual and physical, Bernadette remained strong in character and never swerved from the course shown her by the Immaculate Virgin: to pray and to do penance for sinners.

The final hour had come, and the Sisters knew it. Several gathered by Bernadette's bed; they prayed and helped where they could.

"I'm thirsty," the dying sister whispered hoarsely. A cup was quickly procured, but Bernadette took only a swallow. Then she raised a trembling hand to her forehead and tried hard to make the sign of the cross as perfectly as the Blessed Virgin had taught her.

"Mary, most holy," she murmured, "pray for me...poor sinner...poor sinner...."

The rattle of beads sounded unnaturally loud in the silent room as Bernadette's hand relaxed and her rosary slid gently to the side of the bed. Her pilgrimage was over. Her longing to see the beautiful Lady again was finally satisfied—for now Bernadette would see her eternally. The glorious mysteries of her own life were just beginning...and they would never end.

She could make her own, the words of Mary herself:

"My being proclaims the greatness of the Lord,
my spirit finds joy in God my savior,
For he has looked upon his servant in her
    lowliness...
[he] has done great things for me...."

(Lk. 1:46-48, 49)

34

"no greater love"

Early July in Central Italy is unbearably hot, especially in the region surrounding Nettuno and its neighboring environs, hidden among the marshes and encompassed by an oppressive and unhealthy atmosphere.

That summer day in 1902, there was no means of respite. The sun beat down mercilessly through the malaria-infected air and the heat licked its way across the hard-worked farmland and into the poverty-stricken home of the Goretti and Serenelli families.

Giovanni Serenelli glanced through the open door. "Let's get back to work," he said. "There's a rain cloud on the horizon, and we've still got a lot to do."

Mamma Assunta Goretti heaved a silent sigh and glanced about the room at her children. Perhaps Luigi had been right. Maybe she should have gone back to Corinaldo. The memory of her dead husband's words echoed in her ears: "Assunta, go back to Corinaldo.... Go back to Corinaldo." Poor Luigi, she thought....

Serenelli's quick words and movements brought her back to reality. He had already gathered up some farm implements and was making his way toward the back porch.

Assunta jumped up and followed. The hay and straw were already in the barn, but the beans were still drying in the sun. They had to be gathered up before the rain came.

"Harness the team," Giovanni called to Angelo Goretti and to his own son Alexander.

Angelo went out immediately. The rest of the Goretti children scampered out with him.

Alexander alone remained behind.

Meanwhile, on the other side of the kitchen, twelve-year-old Maria Goretti collected the dishes and began her normal round of household chores.

Maria was unusually mature for her age. Physically, she was attractive and looked three or four years older than she actually was. The full burden of housekeeping and the responsibility of her younger brothers and sisters had fallen on her young shoulders. In the eyes of the townspeople she had proved herself worthy of the trust her mother had placed in her.

Beyond this, there was nothing that distinguished Maria from the other young women of the locality. To everyone, she was a good, hardworking girl whom Assunta Goretti was rearing as any Christian mother should.

Alexander's eyes followed Maria as she worked. He was pensive for a moment. Then he ventured, "Maria, I've got a shirt to be mended. I need it for Mass tomorrow. Fix it for me this afternoon. It's on my bed."

Maria knew very well that Alexander never went to Mass and she suspected something. However, charity prompted otherwise. As soon as she finished the dishes, she got the shirt and settled herself on the porch, with her baby sister, Theresa, sleeping peacefully beside her.

My mother is right, Maria thought. There is something bothering me. But how can I tell her? Alexander threatened to kill me.... Maria broke out in a cold, clammy sweat and her heart pounded furiously. I've got to tell her, she thought. I've got to—but how?... He's approached me twice already and sooner or later he's bound to overpower me. I feel so weak and helpless. O my God, give me the strength and courage I need never to commit sin. My Lord, I'm so afraid...."

Then, suddenly, what she feared most happened. Alexander stood beside her.

"Maria, get in here!"

She sat motionless.

"Get in here! Do you hear me?" He grabbed her by the arm, pulled her into the kitchen and locked the door. There was little hope of escape.

Immediately, she understood his intentions and made a quick, firm decision. "No, Alexander," she screamed, "never!"

By this time, he had his victim firmly pinned to the floor with one knee. "I won't take 'no' for an answer. Give in or I'll kill you!"

"No, no! I won't! It's a sin. God forbids it. Alexander, you will go to hell if you do it!"

His anger turned to uncontrollable rage.

"Alexander, let me go! Let me go!"

He poised a knife over her. There was a moment of silence. One moment in which to choose life or death, sin or martyrdom.

With superhuman courage Maria chose God. "No! Alexander. I won't!"

Time and time again Alexander plunged the knife into the body of his helpless victim. Maria made no attempt to ward off the blows. Then she lost consciousness. The sight of the blood sobered the boy somewhat and he fled from the room.

When Maria came to, she was in an agony of pain. She dragged herself through the pool of her own blood toward the kitchen door. Slowly, she unbolted it and made a feeble effort to call for help.

As soon as Alexander heard her voice, he ran back to the kitchen, grabbed her by the throat and stabbed her clear through six more times. Then he barred himself in his bedroom.

Writhing in pain, Maria lay in that condition for another hour before anyone came back to the house. It was Mr. Serenelli who found her. He called frantically to Maria's mother, who was still working out in the fields. "Assunta, Assunta, come here!"

Poor Mamma Assunta collapsed from the shock. But kind neighbor women immediately set to work.

Maria's clothes were saturated with blood that had congealed and they had to be cut off piece by piece. Yet her lips remained sealed. She would not reveal the name of her assailant. Finally, Mamma Assunta managed to get some information.

"It was Alexander."

"But why?"

"Because I refused to sin."

It was enough. Mamma Assunta pried no further.

Four hours later, a horse-drawn ambulance arrived to carry the brave girl to a hospital in nearby Nettuno. But Maria's ordeal was not over. The surgeons decided to operate with no anesthetics. They found fourteen wounds. Her intestines were torn, her lungs pierced completely through and her heart grazed.

It spite of the stitching and bandaging Maria did not let one cry escape her. She passed the night in sheer torture.

The following morning, however, when the priest brought Holy Communion, her face lit up in ecstatic joy. Jesus had offered up His life for her; now she made an offering of her own life to Him.

Just before Maria received Communion, she turned and fixed her eyes on the crucifix: "I, too, pardon Alexander. I, too, desire that some day he may join me in heaven."

Mamma Assunta wept and so did everyone else in the room. Later that day they discovered black and blue lumps on Maria's knees, legs and arms—all mute testimony to the desperate struggle she had put up.

Maria was going fast—she had blood poisoning; she was hemorrhaging internally; her respiration was failing. Shortly after three o'clock on July 2, 1902— the feast of the Most Precious Blood—Maria surrendered her pure soul to God.

And what of Alexander Serenelli? He served a prison term of some thirty-five years and returned a changed man. On Christmas Eve, 1937, he went to beg pardon of Mamma Assunta.

"Maria forgave you, Alexander," the heroic mother replied. "How could I possibly refuse to?"

The next day Alexander went to the parish church. There, before receiving Holy Communion. he suddenly turned and said to the astonished congregation,

"I have sinned deeply. I murdered an innocent girl who loved virtue more than life. May God forgive me! I beg your pardon!"

Today, the incorrupt body of St. Maria Goretti lies enshrined in a glass urn in the church at Nettuno.

Maria Goretti was neither simple-minded nor ignorant. She was neither insensible to human passions
nor inexperienced in the ways of the world. Her
desperate battle demanded fortitude and courage.
She consciously and freely gave her life rather than
lose the priceless treasure of her virginity.

Rightly did Pope Pius XII pray to her with these
words: "In your virginal countenance may be read
the strength of your love and the constancy of your
fidelity to your divine Spouse. As His bride espoused
in blood, you have traced in yourself His own image."

Maria Goretti had attained the promise of the
Beatitudes: Blessed are the pure of heart, for they
shall see God.

> "The Lord is my light and my salvation;
>   whom should I fear?
> The Lord is my life's refuge;
>   of whom should I be afraid?
> When evildoers come at me
>   to devour my flesh,
> My foes and my enemies
>   themselves stumble and fall.
> Though an army encamp against me,
>   my heart will not fear;
> Though war be waged upon me,
>   even then will I trust.
> One thing I ask of the Lord;
>   this I seek:
> To dwell in the house of the Lord
>   all the days of my life,
> That I may gaze on the loveliness of the Lord
>   and contemplate his temple.
> For he will hide me in his abode
>   in the day of trouble;

He will conceal me in the shelter of his tent,
   he will set me high upon a rock.
Even now my head is held high
   above my enemies on every side.
And I will offer in his tent
   sacrifices with shouts of gladness;
I will sing and chant praise to the Lord."

(Ps. 27:1-6)

Daughters of St. Paul

IN MASSACHUSETTS
    50 St. Paul's Avenue, Boston, Ma. 02130
    172 Tremont Street, Boston, Ma. 02111
IN NEW YORK
    78 Fort Place, Staten Island, N.Y. 10301
    625 East 187th Street, Bronx, N.Y. 10458
    525 Main Street, Buffalo, N.Y. 14203
IN NEW JERSEY
    84 Washington Street, Bloomfield, N.J. 07003
IN CONNECTICUT
    202 Fairfield Avenue, Bridgeport, Ct. 06603
IN OHIO
    2105 Ontario St. (at Prospect Ave.), Cleveland, Oh. 44115
    25 E. Eighth Street, Cincinnati, Oh. 45202
IN PENNSYLVANIA
    1719 Chestnut St., Philadelphia, Pa. 19103
IN FLORIDA
    2700 Biscayne Blvd., Miami, Fl. 33137
IN LOUISIANA
    4403 Veterans Memorial Blvd.,
      Metairie, La. 70002
    86 Bolton Avenue, Alexandria, La. 71301
IN MISSOURI
    1001 Pine St. (at North 10th), St. Louis, Mo. 63101
IN TEXAS
    114 East Main Plaza, San Antonio, Tx. 78205
IN CALIFORNIA
    1570 Fifth Avenue, San Diego, Ca. 92101
    278 17th Street, Oakland, Ca. 94612
    46 Geary Street, San Francisco, Ca. 94108
IN HAWAII
    1184 Bishop St., Honolulu, Hi. 96813
IN ALASKA
    5th Ave. and H. St.
    Anchorage, Ak. 99501
IN CANADA
    3022 Dufferin Street, Toronto 395, Ontario, Canada
IN ENGLAND
    57, Kensington Church Street, London W. 8, England
IN AUSTRALIA
    58, Abbotsford Rd., Homebush, N.S.W., Sydney 2140,
    Australia